THE JEWELRY MAKER'S DESIGN BOOK:
AN ALCHEMY OF OBJECTS

TECHNIQUES AND DESIGN NOTES
FOR ONE-OF-A-KIND JEWELRY PIECES

DERYN MENTOCK

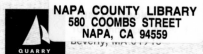

QUARRY

e 406L

Beverly, MA 01915

quarrybooks.com • craftside.typepad.com

This book is dedicated to my wildly creative students. You make teaching a joy!

First published in the United States of America in 2013 by
Quarry Books, a member of
Quarto Publishing Group USA Inc.
100 Cummings Center
Suite 406-L
Beverly, Massachusetts 01915-6101
Telephone: (978) 282-9590
Fax: (978) 283-2742
www.quarrybooks.com
Visit www.Craftside.Typepad.com for a behind-the-scenes peek at our crafty world!

10 9 8 7 6 5 4 3 2

ISBN: 978-1-59253-884-3

Digital edition published in 2014
eISBN: 978-1-61058-935-2

Library of Congress Cataloging-in-Publication Data available

Book Design: meganjonesdesign.com
Cover Image: Deryn Mentock and shutterstock.com
Photography by Deryn Mentock and Alyssa Wible
Illustrations by Trina Dalziel

Printed in China

contents

INTRODUCTION

MY FIXATION WITH JEWELRY began at a very young age. I remember happily digging through my Grandma's little jewelry box, fondling the pop-bead necklaces, and admiring the rhinestone brooches. She didn't have anything expensive, but in my eyes it was treasure. Grandma loved jewelry and passed that love down to my mother, and then to me. Mom is an incredibly creative lady who encouraged me in every art and craft I touched (as did my dad). When I was a kid, we spent many contented hours together sewing, painting, making leaded glass windows, creating jewelry, and antique shopping. She used to take me to the little craft shop in town for beads and findings to be fashioned into earrings. The very first project we made together was a pair of colorful rings, made from plastic-covered telephone wire. Hers was made of gorgeous wire spirals; mine—not so much!

My creative journey was sidetracked later in life by school, work, and eventually my two sons. As fulfilling as these were, a maker-of-things can't give up making things, and that urge came blowing full force back into my life. I discovered collage, assemblage, drawing, bookmaking, and jewelry making all over again. Finally, with a finger in every creative pie, a wise advisor said to me, "Make jewelry, you're good at that!" So be it.

I used to play a game with my kids when they were little. We would go out to find as much parking lot or sidewalk detritus as possible. At the end, we traded junk, and the trading was sometimes fierce! The stuff they found was fascinating, and it was the beginning of my love of found objects. It seemed a natural step to add interesting objects into my jewelry. For me, the options are limitless, and while

Whether I'm making a recipe, a piece of jewelry, or a white-rose-and-jasmine tea or the perfume, I like to think of myself as a happy little sorceress, and if I could just have a little general store with all that stuff and give people a sense of my taste, that would be lovely.

—PADMA LAKSHMI

I've added more sophisticated objects into the mix, I still find that the combination of found and fabricated material is magical.

Over the years I've taken classes, practiced my skills, and discovered a passion for teaching and design. This book combines three of my biggest jewelry-making obsessions: technical skills, design, and found objects. Good technique and design are absolutely essential to beautiful jewelry. Over the years I've found that many of my students struggle with both, and especially with design.

My sincere desire with this book is to share with you some of what I've learned. I keep a jewelry journal filled with my design ideas and sketches, and this book is a more detailed extension of that. I mean to offer you a glimpse of what I do and how I do it—to invite you into my artistic world and allow you to see my creative process. I want you to believe you can do it too. We will explore the magic of sublime design and the fundamental ways in which elements relate to each other—in other words, the alchemy of objects!

A designer knows he has achieved perfection not when there is
nothing left to add, but when there is nothing left to take away.

—ANTOINE DE SAINT-EXUPÉRY

CHAPTER 1

DESIGN ALCHEMY

THE LANGUAGE OF DESIGN: ELEMENTS AND PRINCIPLES FOR JEWELRY MAKERS

Is your work well made but missing that special something? Nothing is more important to making beautiful jewelry than good design. Strong skills and good techniques are crucial to creating quality pieces, and if design excellence is missing, your efforts will fall flat. Brilliant design makes the difference between a nice piece of jewelry and an inspiring piece of jewelry that pops.

Like any other art form, beauty is in the eye of the beholder. Handmade jewelry is a personal expression from the artist's hands, and the viewer's experience of it is a subjective matter. Different people are drawn to different styles, colors, and types of jewelry; superior design will make your piece of jewelry stand out. Jewelry design is a visual language that once learned, will help you express your creative vision.

Strong design, translated through excellent techniques, is what defines your personal style, and allows you to express that style in your own unique artistic voice. Learning and understanding the elements and principles of design will allow you to create a much stronger statement.

elements

Elements are the physical aspects of a design; the structure, parts, and components that make up a piece of jewelry. These are what the viewer first observes, and they define the jewelry maker's message. The way the parts are arranged, as well as the physical properties of the individual components (found objects, beads, links, wirework, metalwork) is vital to a successful design. Elements are the words in the language of design. The message of your jewelry will be conveyed through a good understanding of this language: shape, size, space, color, and texture.

SHAPE

Shape is what many people first see when viewing jewelry.

Contrast and excitement are created when varied shapes are included within a piece. Alternatively, consistent shapes can serve as a low-key background for a fascinating focal point. Jewelry can be simple yet interesting, and well designed merely from the visual impact of the shapes used.

SIZE

Size refers to the dimensions of the elements used in a piece of jewelry. Varying the sizes of objects within a piece can create an interesting tension or calming harmony. For instance, if one element is larger than the others, the eye will be immediately drawn to the larger shape. Many elements that are the same size and shape create a more fluid and calming

message to the viewer. Varied sizes within the piece can add interest and contrast. Size should be considered when combining components so the end result is harmonious and in proportion.

Size also refers to the scale of the jewelry as a whole. When designing, it is important to consider the wearer. The finished piece should be proportionate to the person it is designed for—the piece should be wearable.

SPACE

Positive space (full) is the space occupied by an object, while negative space (empty) is the area surrounding the positive space. The space around and between objects affects the way the objects relate to each other and is an important aspect of viewing

the jewelry as a whole. Negative space is just as important as positive space and can provide the eye with a resting place in a busy design.

COLOR

The element of color is one of the most obvious and powerful design tools. Learning to use a color wheel will help you immensely when making color selections for your designs.

Primary colors include red, yellow, and blue. Secondary colors are orange, green, and purple, and are created by mixing primary colors. Tertiary colors are created when a primary color is mixed with a secondary color. With the help of a color wheel, you'll be able to combine colors into specific color schemes, which enables you to use color in a pleasing way. For example, a complementary color scheme uses two colors that are opposite each other on the color wheel, creating a high contrast combination.

There are a few other terms, which are useful to know when discussing color. *Hue* is 100-percent pure saturated color. *Value* is the lightness or darkness of a color. *Contrast* is the difference between light and dark. *Tint* is a hue (or color) to which white has been added. *Shade* is a hue to which black has been added. *Tone* is a hue to which grey has been added. All of these terms play a part in color theory and are useful tools in good jewelry design. Learning how to use color to your benefit can make all the difference to your work.

TEXTURE

Texture adds dimension and interest, and it is apparent in all works whether it is rough, smooth, hard, or soft. Texture can be classified into two categories: physical and visual. Physical texture can be seen and felt—it is the smoothness of a lovely stone, the hard edge of forged metal, or the textural properties of a found object. Visual texture is the illusion of physical texture and can be emphasized with the materials you use. Sparkle is a great example of visual texture; a rhinestone brooch or faceted stone provides visual texture.

PRINCIPLES

Principles are the organizational components of design. If elements are the words in design language, then principles are the way the words are arranged. Principles are the invisible concepts that make or break a good design, and include emphasis, balance, rhythm, proportion, and unity.

EMPHASIS AND FOCUS

Emphasis forces the eye to focus on a dominant element. That element may be an object, or it may be a design element, such as color. There should be a point of emphasis in every piece of jewelry that you create—it is what draws the eye. If there are too many points of emphasis, the eye becomes confused—the jewelry will lack harmony, be unattractive, and difficult to view. On the other hand, if there is no point of emphasis, the piece may lack interest and not hold the viewer's attention.

BALANCE

Balance refers to the visual weight of the jewelry. It can be symmetrical, meaning equally balanced with an even distribution of components on each side,

or it can be asymmetrical with an uneven distribution. Symmetrical balance gives a more formal, stable feel and is easily achieved by using a focal point with elements placed evenly on either side. Asymmetrical balance involves visual weight that is equal but not exactly the same, and lends a more informal, spontaneous feel. The physical weight of an asymmetrical design must be balanced to ensure the jewelry hangs correctly.

PROPORTION

Proportion is the comparative relationship between components

and elements. It is the way each object's size, shape, color, and texture relate to each other and to the piece as a whole. Good proportion adds harmony and balance to jewelry. If the proportion of one element is off, the balance of the design will be disrupted, and the eye will be drawn to the wrong place.

RHYTHM AND MOVEMENT

Rhythm is the way the eye moves over the work. The eye should be drawn in by a focal point, travel easily over the lesser points of emphasis, and then around the piece. Rhythm is created when

elements are repeated, thus creating movement and energy.

UNITY AND HARMONY

Unity is the harmonious combination of all parts into an esthetically satisfying whole. Unity does not necessarily mean that all of the parts match, but rather that they go together. Without unity, a design can be chaotic and the viewer will not be engaged.

WEARABILITY

Some pieces of art jewelry are not designed to be worn daily and are considered showpieces. Alternatively, there is functional jewelry. When a piece of jewelry will be worn regularly your workmanship should be impeccable; there should be no sharp edges, loose wires, or anything that could cut or poke the wearer. The piece should hang properly without having to be adjusted. Weight is a consideration as well. A necklace that is too heavy can be uncomfortable. Wearing jewelry should be a joy, not an annoyance.

DURABILITY

Durability is an important factor in jewelry design. I construct my pieces to last and you should as well. There should be no loose jump rings or other connections. All elements should be strongly secured so nothing is lost during the wearing and handling of the piece. Strung beads should be completely secured with good crimps, and solder joins should be strong and durable. You don't want one of your pieces to come apart while it is being worn.

a few common mistakes

When I teach, I come into contact with jewelry makers of all levels, and over the years I've seen some design and technical mistakes that are made repeatedly.

- LESS IS MORE: One of the most common errors I see is trying to combine too many elements, physical or visual, into a design. As more elements are added, the piece suffers as a whole. Not every object, design element, and principle need be emphasized in one piece of jewelry. For instance, if color is a dominant element, it should be used judiciously. Typically, I use no more than two or three different colors in one piece, but I may add interest by using many different shades, tints, or tones of those colors.

- LACK OF FOCUS: Often there is an inclination to include every favorite bead and object into one design. Elements that take too much attention away from the focus should not be included. When adding objects try this—look at the piece with the new object, and then look at it without the object. Does the new object add to the piece, take away from the piece, or do nothing? Does the object distract from the focal point? If it does anything but enhance the overall work, it should not be included.

- POOR WORKMANSHIP: Your jewelry should never go out into the world without proper finishing. This relates directly to wearability, but impeccably finished work also looks more beautiful and professional. For example, edges should be smooth so that they don't catch on clothing or scratch the wearer. Ear wires should always be finished so they are smooth and bur-free on the ends. Charms and dangles should be attached securely. Attention to this kind of detail is crucial, especially if you will be selling your jewelry.

- POOR DESIGN: Developing outstanding technical skills takes many hours of practice, and exceptional design skills take just as much time and effort. Beginning students sometimes feel great frustration when these things don't come immediately, but perfecting your craft takes time and work. If jewelry making is your passion, invest the time and practice to create and design quality pieces.

- NOT READY FOR PRIME TIME: I see many students anxious to jump into business and begin selling their work before they are truly ready. Take the time to perfect your skills as well as develop your own style. Allow your skills to grow and your style to mature, and your pieces will attract the attention they deserve.

Developing a Personal Jewelry-making Style

Every jewelry designer wants his or her work to be unique and noticed. To achieve that, it is vital to develop your own style. If you are just beginning, you probably haven't had enough time to develop the important technical skills, let alone a unique style. But once you are past the initial learning phase, you will want your work to reflect your own spirit. This is essential if you want to sell your jewelry. Your work should communicate your voice so when people see your jewelry, they think of your name, not another artist's.

One of the ways to cultivate a unique style is to develop your skills, and the only way to do that is by practice, practice, practice. And when you think you have done enough, practice some more! The number of techniques you know means nothing if they are done in a haphazard way. Learn the best techniques for the pieces you have in mind. Your work should be well designed, perfectly executed, and professionally finished—especially if you are thinking of selling your jewelry. Find an instructor or two that you like, and take some classes. At first your workmanship may not be of the same as an experienced jewelery maker, but don't get discouraged. As your skills and techniques improve, you will see an evolution of your personal style. Nothing should leave your studio that isn't excellent quality and without the mark of your own creative voice.

WHAT ATTRACTS YOU?

Take the time to reflect on the types of jewelry, materials, and styles you are drawn to. Are you interested in antique elements and found objects? Or, are you attracted to modern, sleek lines? Do you enjoy organic materials; beads, metals, fibers, and stones? Also examine the themes and styles that interest you: romantic, Native American, grunge, Victorian, and techno are just a few. There are many types of jewelry to choose from as well as different mediums: wire working, metal clay, fiber jewelry, found-object jewelry, traditional jewelry making, glass jewelry, polymer, and more. Are there symbols, lines, shapes, or words that have meaning for you? Incorporating personal stories and messages into your work will give your work a personal tone

MENTORSHIP

Find a mentor, or several mentors. Look for someone willing to give you honest and objective feedback on the good, bad, and ugly in your work. Constructive criticism is helpful not only when it comes to your work but also in regards to business decisions, professional relationships, and general support. Obviously the best mentor would be someone who has more experience, who motivates you, and is inspiring. Over time your jewelry style will change, your skills will improve, and your inner exceptional style will emerge.

and become a part of your style expression. Giving all of these things some serious thought, and focusing on what speaks to you, will help you develop your jewelry style.

Good design is critical for sense of style in your jewelry. You must consider careful placement of elements, composition, focal point, movement, shape, size, texture, use of color, and materials in every piece. Once you learn how to apply these principles, you will see a big difference—not only in the way your pieces look but also how you feel about your work. Using good design principles enables your style to shine through.

DEVELOPING CONCEPTS: FINDING INSPIRATION AND KEEPING A JEWELRY JOURNAL

If you have ever experienced a creative block, you know that inspiration can be elusive and fleeting. The original meaning of inspiration is "to inspire, to inflame, blow into ... to breathe," "the immediate influence of God or a god." Modern day inspiration is defined as "an arousal of the mind." It is that feeling that awakens excitement and stimulates us into meaningful creative action. It is the very beginning of an idea, and it can come from anywhere.

One of my most important creative tools is my jewelry journal—my design bible. If you don't keep a design journal, you may want to start one. It is a great place to jot down ideas before they slip away. You think you will remember your ideas, but most of us don't! Writing helps us to recall and solidify thoughts. Sketching also helps the design process by working through any problems. You may never make a piece of jewelry from those sketches, but they may inspire other ideas.

Your jewelry journal can be simple or fancy—a leftover composition notebook, or a handmade and

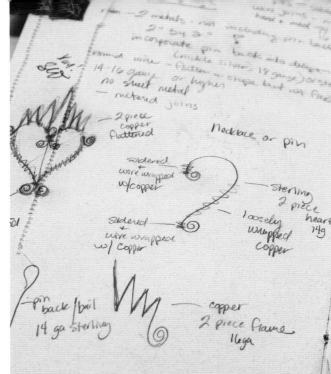

collaged book. Keep your jewelry sketchbook handy to record your ideas as soon as they come. I travel with mine, but I also keep it in my studio to write down measurements and steps for pieces that I am working on. If something triggers a design idea, I sketch it in my jewelry journal. If I see an image I find intriguing, I cut it out and glue it in my journal. I use my journal for color swatches and to work out color palettes. I use it to record reference information for supply and bead sources. It is also a good place to keep contact cards, notes from other artists, and teaching notes.

If I'm feeling uninspired I will sit and flip through the pages of my journal and inevitably find ideas that I have forgotten about. I don't always have time to immediately work on an idea when it comes to mind, but if it is in my journal, I can always refer to it later. Just looking through the pages of my jewelry journal helps get me out of a creative rut, and drawing out my thoughts and ideas is the first step toward creating something wonderful.

If you are not terrific at drawing, don't let that stop you from keeping a journal. You don't have to draw perfectly. The most important thing is to get your ideas out of your head and onto the paper. Doodling and recording design thoughts will help prompt the creative process. Use your journal as a safe place to ask yourself "what if?" Draw different versions of a design; try it with alternate color schemes or construction methods. Allow yourself to sketch freely in your design journal, and do it frequently to help keep you in that creative design zone.

JUMPSTART YOUR CREATIVITY

Typically, inspiration comes from things to which we are attracted. If you find yourself feeling less than creative, there are several things you can try to arouse your mind and get back on track.

- Go for a walk. Take your camera for impromptu shots and capture anything that grabs your attention. There may be a shape or color in a photo that sparks an idea for a new design.

- Take a break from jewelry making. It sometimes helps to delve into a medium in which you don't typically work. Play with collage or paints, create an assemblage, or pick up a sewing project.

- Listen to music. Turn on your favorite tunes, or listen to different types of music. Music and lyrics can often inspire a chain of ideas.

- Go shopping. For me, one of the best ways to trigger ideas is to go antique shopping. Even if I don't buy anything, vendors often display their wares in decorative and inspiring ways.

- Clean your studio. During the process you may run across forgotten beads or objects that are begging to be used. As an added bonus, a clean studio is much easier to work in!

- Practice your techniques. It never hurts to practice, and working through some of the techniques may bring on new ideas.

THE OBJECTS

TREASURE HUNT: WHERE TO GO AND WHAT TO LOOK FOR

I have always been a treasure hunter. I grew up antiquing and going to garage sales with my mom, who is a tenacious collector of good "junque." These hunter-gatherer tendencies have proven very beneficial to my career as a found-object jewelry designer. You can find items everywhere. Always keep your eyes open for items you can use—over the years I have developed a nice stash of beads, stones, and objects.

There are many opportunities to find objects for jewelry designing when you include the Internet. Auction sites and online marketplaces are overflowing with trash and treasures. Search a little and you should be able to find what you are looking for.

Antique malls are great places to find vintage and antique elements. Take your time and don't pass up the glass-enclosed cases. Most vendors keep small things locked up, but don't hesitate to ask to see something. Antiques can be expensive, but if you find something you like, make an offer. Many dealers are willing to barter when it comes to the price.

If you are lucky enough to live near a flea market, put on some comfortable shoes, and get ready to browse. Also make sure to take some cash in case a vendor doesn't take credit cards.

When purchasing vintage or antique objects, make sure to examine them closely for any damage. Some wear and tear and a lovely aged patina are bonuses in my book, but the item must be useable and sturdy enough to use in jewelry making. Also consider broken pieces, as they can be invaluable for parts. Keep in mind how you intend to attach the item. If you can't make an attachment without causing damage, you may want to pass up the piece. Be aware of the weight; it may be too heavy to use for jewelry. Also consider that what you find could be valuable. If you buy a vintage rhinestone brooch for $30 and discover it is worth $300, you may be happy you didn't alter it to use in your found-object necklace.

WORKING WITH, REPAIRING, AND MODIFYING OBJECTS

BEADS
Gemstone beads and pearls can have very small holes. If I need to enlarge the holes I use an electric bead reamer with a diamond tip—well worth the small investment. Make sure you ream the hole with the drill tip slightly underwater to keep it cool.

RHINESTONES
If you like using vintage rhinestone pieces in your jewelry, you will find that many are missing rhinestones. For me, that adds to the charm and it doesn't

bother me to use them with a few missing stones. However, if you want to replace missing stones you can easily find new stones to purchase, or look for vintage jewelry to use for stone replacement. I seem to end up with lots of loose rhinestones and keep them in my stash to use when I can.

I have a collection of vintage jewelry boxes for storing my rhinestone pieces. This keeps them from banging against each other, which might cause the stones to fall out. If a rhinestone piece is prone to losing its stones, I will store it in a sealed plastic bag—when I am ready to use it, the stones will be there, and ready to be glued back in place.

ROSARIES AND RELIGIOUS MEDALS

I am always on the lookout for vintage rosaries and religious medals, which are getting harder to find and more expensive. I buy them in good condition, and also purchase them in parts. When working with these pieces, especially the vintage variety, be aware that the metal links can be weak or brittle depending on their condition. Open the links to the side, if possible, and work them as little as necessary. Also, make sure that all the links are completely closed when you add rosary parts and religious medals to your work.

PATINA

I rarely use metal in my work that doesn't have an aged look.

If the metal is new, I use a patina solution, or a heat patina to give it character. For sterling or copper, a liver-of-sulfur patina works very well and is safe to use. I use a liver-of-sulfur solution on my wire and patina the entire roll at once. Then I clean the wire with a sanding block, manicure stick, or 0000 steel wool as I work.

To age brass and some other metals, use a chemical such as Black Max or Novacan. Novacan is a patina used by stained-glass artists and is nice because it will darken solder. Black Max and Novacan should be used cautiously; follow the instructions on the package, use gloves, and provide good ventilation.

I like to use a heat patina on brass because it is so easy. Sometimes, quickly quenching it in water will give you colorful results. This type of patina must be sealed with a micro wax or another sealer. Soft metals, such as pot metal that many vintage rhinestone pieces are made with, should not be heated. Pewter is also too soft for heating with a torch.

Patina solutions should not be used on dark annealed steel wire. I clean my steel wire by running it between two fine-grit foam sanding blocks before working with it. The wire can be sealed with a micro wax or other sealer, and if you keep the wire dry you shouldn't have any problems with rust.

TINTYPES

Most of the tintypes I use are the small "gem" size. They are old and require a bit of special handling to keep the emulsion from flaking off. I use metal shears to cut them, which sometimes causes flaking. To avoid this, first spray the tintypes with two or three coats of acrylic sealer, or try coating them with an acrylic gel medium.

FABRIC

I keep a small stash of fabric, tatting, ribbon, lace, sari silk ribbon, leather, and other textiles handy to use when I need them. It is sometimes necessary to back a focal with fabric to make it more wearable. Collect scraps at garage sales, fabric stores, and hobby shops. The fabrics I use most often are vintage bark cloth, upholstery fabric, velvet, and leather. I also love recycled sari silk ribbon; the colors are fabulous. When I use fabric objects, such as religious détentes, or leather that requires sewing, I like to use upholstery thread or outdoor thread for its strength.

DRILLING THROUGH OBJECTS

Shells, rocks, porcelain, glass, doll arms, china, bone, antlers, pearls, or any other hard items that create dust and heat up when you are drilling, have to

be drilled underwater. Use a shallow plastic dish and just enough water to cover your item. You will need to use a diamond bit, and the water keeps everything from getting too hot. Some dust is dangerous to breathe, such as that from pearls or shells. Wear safety glasses, and take your time. If you are drilling an object without water, such as cured resin, plastic, or wood, make sure to wear an appropriate dust mask.

RESIN

I use a lot of resin in my work, and I recommend a two-part resin. I like ICE Resin because it is a jewelry-grade product with very little smell, and it cures very clear and hard. Resin can be used to fill bezels or create a clear, durable coating on papers, and it can also be used as an adhesive. Carefully follow the instructions on the package for proper curing.

Beads and Stones: Where to Find, What to Look For, and Storage

When it comes to beads and stones, the infinite choice of colors, shapes, and textures are a terrific opportunity to add interest and variety to your jewelry. They can have a significant impact on the cohesiveness of your designs. The surface of beads and stones (faceted, smooth, and rough) adds physical texture, while color and pattern add visual texture and impact. Crystals and druzy stones add visual texture in the form of sparkle, and are a great way to add a dash of texture and excitement.

I often shop antique malls and flea markets for found objects, and while I'm there I keep an eye out for interesting vintage beads. Shopping the Internet is an easy way to find beads without ever leaving home. Make sure you use a bead gauge when shopping online as photos can be deceiving when it comes to bead sizes. I also occasionally shop at my local bead shop.

My favorite venue for bead shopping is gem-and-bead shows—the selection and prices can't be beat. Most shows are large and the choices can be overwhelming. Before you leave home think about the jewelry projects you are currently working on, and make a list of the sizes, shapes, colors, and textures you're looking for.

STORAGE

Once you have collected a stash of beads, stones, and objects, you need a good way to organize them. I keep my beads in lidded plastic storage boxes with fixed dividers. I separate my beads by color and label the outside of each box so I can easily access the color I need when designing. Anything fragile is kept separate to prevent chipping or breaking. I use separate boxes for pearls, which are also labeled by color.

Cabochons (cabs) are flat on the bottom and are usually used in a bezel setting. I collect them in various colors, shapes, and sizes. These are stored separately from the beads and pearls in plastic divided boxes.

Heavy Metal: Metals and Wire

Sheet metal and wire are sold in various gauges; the smaller the gauge, the heavier the metal or wire (see photo, right). I like to keep a variety of metal and wire in various gauges so it is available when I need it. I love the look of mixed metals and gauges and don't hesitate to combine them, but I do have a few rules. I always use 20-gauge sterling for ear wires; it is the most comfortable and most people aren't allergic to it. I do not use steel for bracelets or rings because it can rust if it comes in contact with moisture. Purchase a wire gauge and use it; you will soon become familiar with the different thicknesses.

I store most of my wire in a worm binder (see photo, page 25, left), which is like a three-ring binder with large resealable bags for easy organization. You can buy extra bags and mark them for different gauges. Worm binders can be found at sporting good stores.

- Sterling is a lovely metal. It is easily annealed and easy to work with. I like to use it for all kinds of projects, especially high-end pieces. I buy dead soft, which means it is easier to work with. Sterling wire, even the heavier gauge, is fairly easy to ball with the butane torches I recommend.

- Nickel silver is a good alternative to sterling, although it is much stiffer to work with.
- Copper is softer than nickel but stiffer than sterling. It is a great alternative if you need a low-priced metal for practicing techniques. Heavy gauge copper wire is fairly easy to ball with the butane torches, but not as easy as sterling. When copper is worn very close to the skin, as with rings, it tends to turn the skin green, so I don't use it for ring shanks.
- Brass comes in various alloys that can affect its color and can have a yellow or reddish tint. It is a bit stiffer to work with than copper.

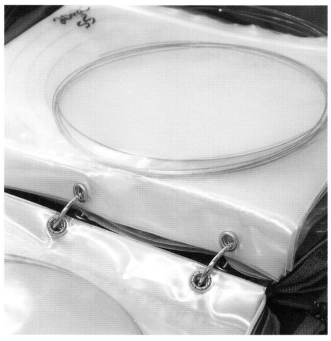

- True bronze is a bit of a different alloy from brass and has a gold-red color. It is even stiffer than brass. There is a lot of information online regarding various percentages of metals used for bronze and brass.
- When I use steel, it is black annealed steel wire. It comes with a black, greasy coating to keep it from rusting on the shelf. I clean the coating off as I work by running it between two sanding blocks. Steel will rust if it comes into contact with too much moisture, but I wear my steel-wire jewelry and have never had a problem with it rusting. Steel is also a great practice wire because it is very inexpensive; however, it is very stiff to work with, and I use the smaller gauges for most applications.

- Because of the low cost, I frequently use copper or brass sheets (see photo above). I use a lot of 24-gauge sheet metal because it is thin enough to cut with metal shears, which saves the time it takes to use a jeweler's saw. For thicker gauges you will still want to use the saw. Any sheet metal 26-gauge, or thinner, is considered craft metal and isn't thick enough to stand up to jewelry making—however, the choice depends on the project. If you are layering, you may need a thin-gauge metal. For higher-end projects I would use sterling sheet. Be careful—sheet metal can have very sharp edges.

SHOPPING TIPS

- SIZE: Let your jewelry style dictate the size of beads you purchase. If you typically work small, then you will gravitate to smaller beads and stones. I like to keep a variety of sizes on hand because I make a wide variety of pieces. For instance, if I am designing earrings, I know the beads should be smaller to reduce the weight. Keep wearability and proportion in mind when considering size.

- SHAPE: Watch for interesting shapes that you may not usually work with. Some standard bead shapes I keep in my stash are round, briolette, and oval. Also notice how the beads are drilled—center drilled (through the middle, up and down) or top drilled (across the top).

- COLOR: Great jewelry design is affected by color. Take a color wheel to easily see classic color combinations, and determine which schemes you might like to use. Is there a color, or two, that you typically work with when making jewelry? I buy strands in similar color groups, and find I have quite a few blues and greens in my stash. Also buy a few colors outside of what you normally use; they will come in handy as accents. When I see a strand or two I can't resist, I usually end up taking them home. I know I will use them sooner or later.

- TEXTURE: A very important aspect of my work is texture, and I am always drawn to imperfect, roughly cut stones, irregular facets, fossils, crystals, and anything unusual. Adding texture to your work is like adding a dash of salt to a good meal; just the right amount enhances perfectly. Beads and stones offer lots of opportunities to add both physical and visual texture to your work.

- QUALITY: Beads and stones come in a wide range of quality. For me, the look of lower-quality faceted stones is what I like to see in my work, and the price is right. High quality stones are usually expensive, but occasionally I will splurge. If you decide to work with only high quality beads and stones, you may want to build your collection slowly. Compare the strands when you are shopping and avoid strands with broken or missing stones, or ask for a discount.

- KNOW YOUR STONES: Many stones are dyed or treated. For example, most turquoise is treated to add stability, as it is a very soft stone. Turquoise can come from the American Southwest (a more expensive stone), China (a less expensive stone), or other countries. Some turquoise is dyed to enhance the color. Some dealers are selling dyed howlite, or more commonly magnesite, as turquoise and should make this clear to the buyer. It is a good idea to study stones, a bit, to know what you are buying. If the stone is treated, but you like what you see, that is all right. If you are a purist and only accept untreated and/or perfect stones and gems, you will pay more for them.

- PEARLS: Pearls come in various qualities and many colors. Colored pearls are usually dyed. The better the pearly finish, or nacre, the better quality the pearl. Quality pearls are usually smooth, uniform in shape and size, and have a lovely finish. There is a world of information to learn about pearls. I usually choose the more imperfect ones, and select the size and shape according to my design idea.

- PRICE: It is easy to get carried away, so set a budget. Many of the large shows also charge for admission and parking. Check the Internet for coupons and sign up for their mailing list. Some of the shows will mail you a coupon for free admission.

- SHOPPING THE SHOWS: If you do decide to shop the large bead shows, wear great walking shoes, and take a backpack, rolling bag, or cart for your purchases. Don't forget to take your business ID, if you have one, as well as your credit card and checkbook—most vendors will take either form of payment. Also take a bit of cash for incidentals and parking.

Practice means to perform, over and over again in the face of all obstacles, some act of vision, of faith, of desire. Practice is a means of inviting the perfection desired.

—MARTHA GRAHAM

CHAPTER 2

Techniques and TOOLS

MATERIALS AND TOOLS

I am not a perfectionist in many aspects of my work, but technique is one thing that I insist be done well. Your work will be much higher quality if you practice and perfect your techniques and finishing skills. That doesn't mean every piece you create has to be filled with complicated techniques or be brought to a mirror finish. Each piece speaks its own language, and that language will be more beautiful if you know what you are doing!

If you are a beginning jewelry maker, you will need to get at least enough tools to practice the basic techniques. I always tell my students to get what they can afford. But if jewelry making is going to be a long-term obsession, invest in some quality tools. Tools are like almost anything; you get what you pay for. High-quality tools really do make a difference in the quality of your work, and you will find them much easier to work with.

JEWELRY PLIERS

The jewelry pliers I find indispensable are extra-long round-nose, round-nose, chain-nose, and flat (see A). None of these pliers should have teeth, which would scratch the metal. I most often use the chain-nose and round-nose pliers. Chain-nose pliers are for bending, shaping, and holding. Round-nose pliers are only for making loops—don't try to use them for anything else! Extra-long round-nose pliers are great if you need a larger loop than what the round-nose can give you. Flat pliers are also for shaping and bending.

Narrow-nose pliers are also called *toothed pliers* because they have teeth (see B). They are heavy-duty, and I use them for many things. These pliers are great for holding wire or metal in a flame, and for working with steel wire.

Bailing pliers are used for shaping and making various-size loops and bends (see C). They are terrific for making clasps, ear wires, and a multitude of other components.

JEWELRY HAMMERS, BENCH BLOCK, AND BENCH PILLOW

There are many, many hammer styles and brands to choose from. The hammers I use the most are *planishing*, *ball-peen*, and *chasing* hammers (see D). Planishing hammers are used to move, shape, form, and smooth metal. Chasing hammers have a large face that is used for striking chasing tools, but I use mine like a planishing hammer—for general hammering. The ball end of the chasing hammer is great for setting eyelets and making rivets. My ball-peen hammer is the typical hardware store variety. I use it mostly for working with steel wire.

Dead-blow, *nylon*, and *rawhide* hammers are used for hardening wire and metal (see E). They are also used for shaping and forming. The surface of these hammers allows for hammering metal without marring. My favorite is a dead-blow hammer, but the others work as well.

You will need a steel bench block or an anvil for making jewelry. Do yourself a favor and don't get one of the big flat types; they are horrible for your hearing! All you really need is a very small surface area. Set the block or anvil on a good bench pillow to cushion the sound; a folded towel works, but not as well.

CUTTING TOOLS

Metal shears are used for cutting through metal. I find that the style shown fits my hand and will cut through small- to medium-gauge metal (see F). You can spend a lot of money on *flush cutters*; I use the cheapest ones and throw them out when they get dull or marred. Flush cutters make a beautiful flat cut and will cut through 16-gauge steel wire. *Power flush cutters* are great to use with found objects for a variety of tasks, such as cutting through pin backs or other thick objects.

A.

B.

C.

D.

E.

F.

G.

H.

I.

J.

K.

L.

FILES AND SANDING SURFACES

Files can be expensive, but if you take care of them, they should last a long, long time. I have a collection of files, and the ones I use most often are a half-round number 0, a half-round number 2, and my needle files. The larger *jewelry files* are great for removing a lot of metal. The *needle files* are for getting into tight spaces. I also use a small set of diamond-coated files. My favorite finishing surfaces are *fine-grit foam sanding blocks* and *manicure pads* (see G); 0000 steel wool does the same job as manicure pads.

WIRE ROUNDER AND CUP BUR

A *wire rounder* is a must-have tool for rounding and smoothing the ends of ear wires. A *cup bur* does the same thing but is used in a flex-shaft or *Dremel-style tool* (see H).

DRILLING TOOLS

I mostly use a *flex-shaft tool* for drilling, but a Dremel-type tool works as well. I like titanium bits because they are strong, and *bit lubricant* helps keep the drill bits cool. Use the *toothed pliers* to hold the object to be drilled, and always use *safety glasses* with power tools (see I).

Many pearls and beads have very small holes and an *electric bead reamer* is the essential tool for enlarging them (see J). It is one of those tools I thought I would never use, but I couldn't do without it.

A *Japanese screw punch* is used for making holes, and is especially good for making holes in leather (see K).

An *awl* is good for marking metal, expanding holes, or picking up tiny eyelets. Use a *center punch* for marking metal before drilling, and as an eyelet setter (see L).

BUTANE TORCHES

For the projects in this book, you will need two small *butane torches*. The larger torch burns hotter and is used for annealing metal and balling the ends of heavy-gauge wire. The smaller torch is used for balling smaller-gauge wire and can be used for soft soldering (see M). They are easy to fill and take up very little space on your workbench. Always wear *safety glasses* when using a torch.

BENCH VISES

Vises are used for holding metal and wire, and for making rivets. The small *bench vise* is good for when you travel (see N).

HOOP MANDREL

A *hoop mandrel* is used for forming metal and is terrific for making earrings and large hoops (see O).

EYELETS

Eyelets are handy to use in place of making tube rivets (see P).

SEWING TOOLS

If you need to make repairs on a fabric focal or hand stitch beads or notions in place, a sturdy thread is best. I use *upholstery thread* in most cases. *Tapestry needles* come in a variety of sizes and work well for leather (see Q).

BEADING TOOLS

For strength I like to use flexible *beading wire* in either fine or medium. One strand of this beading wire is made up of multiple strands of wire, which is coated by plastic so it is very strong. I use 2 mm sterling *crimp tubes* in the appropriate size for the wire I am using. My favorite crimper is the *Magical Crimping Tool* (see R), but other crimpers work well, including the type that crimps in one step. *Bead stoppers* are extremely helpful for keeping beads on the wire during stringing (see S).

ADHESIVES AND WAX

In some situations it is necessary to use an adhesive. I use *white glue* for general things, such as adhering an image into a bezel before filling it with resin. *Gel medium* is used to coat images before placing them into a bezel, which will then be filled with resin. When I need to replace a rhinestone in a piece of vintage jewelry I use *jewelry cement*. *Micro wax mediums* are good for sealing a patina on metal (see T).

COLOR WHEEL

A *color wheel* is an essential design tool (see U). It will help you see which colors go well together and which don't. It is an important tool for planning color schemes and seeing shades, tints, and tones of various colors.

M.

N.

O.

P.

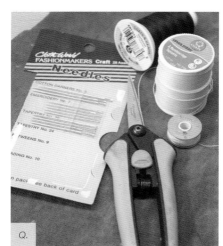

Q.

R.

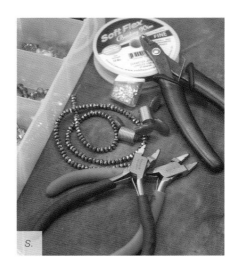

S.

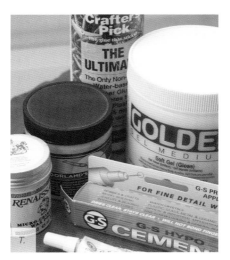

T.

U.

WORKING SAFELY WITH METAL

It is best to practice safety first when it comes to working with tools, torches, and chemicals. For the most part, jewelry making is a fairly safe adventure. The following are a few general tips to be aware of:

· Always wear safety glasses when working with power tools, chemicals, or a torch. You only have one pair of eyes; make sure to protect them.

· When cutting wire, cover the end with your finger and point the end down toward the workbench. Tiny bits of cut wire can fly with amazing velocity and do a lot of damage if they come into contact with an eye.

· When soldering or working with chemicals, make sure you have proper ventilation. It is best to have an exhaust system that vents to the outside, or work outside or in a garage with a large open door.

· Wear a protective apron. If you are working with chemicals, always also wear protective gloves and safety glasses.

· Wear a dust mask any time you are doing a task that creates dust, such as filing, sanding, or enameling.

· Don't eat or drink when you are working. It is easy for debris to fall into your food or drink.

· Always wash your hands thoroughly when you are finished working.

· Don't wear loose, flowing clothing or jewelry, and tie back long hair while you're working—especially when working with power tools.

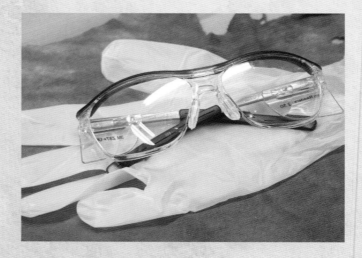

· When hammering, keep anything off the bench block that you would rather not have smashed.

· Be aware of your materials, tools, and surroundings.

TORCH SAFETY

These tips apply when using handheld gas torches such as butane, MAPP gas, or propane. For the most part I use two sizes of small butane torches and/or a MAPP gas torch. Although these torches are small and easy to use, they still reach very high temperatures, and should be handled carefully. Please use the following precautions:

· Use a ceramic tile or metal tray under your torch, even when using a solder board. If you use a charcoal block, place it atop a solder board.

- Arrange your tools so you are not reaching in front of the flame, and make sure the area in front of the flame is clear. When a Boy Scout is holding a knife in his hand, the area his arm can reach is called his "blood circle," and he is required to make sure there is no one inside this circle. Consider the area your flame can reach your "blood circle"!

- Make sure you have everything you need for the job before you start.

- Tie back hair, loose clothing, and jewelry.

- Have your quench water ready in a heat-proof container. Also keep a fire extinguisher nearby and know how to use it.

- Always wear eye protection. Water, flux, and steel-wool bits can sputter and fly. Protect your eyes from hot flying debris.

- Make sure you have proper ventilation.

- Keep a hand on the torch when it is lit whenever possible.

- Play it safe and consider everything at your torch station to be hot. Don't forget that the nozzle of your torch, the pliers holding your metal, and your solder block hold heat and can burn you.

- When you are finished using the torch, turn it off! Don't leave a burning torch sitting; it is extremely easy to knock it over.

- When the torch is lit, give it your full focus and respect. Don't allow distractions when using the torch.

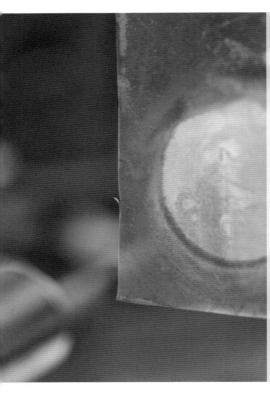

annealing metal

Anneal metal or wire before working with it to soften and make it easier to manipulate. As you work with the annealed metal, it will regain its stiffness. Anneal again as needed.

TOOLS

· toothed pliers
· torch

MATERIALS

· metal or wire

1. Hold the metal or wire securely with pliers and move it slowly through the torch flame until it glows a dull orange. Then move immediately to the next section of metal.

2. Quench it in water.

DRawInG a BEaD on WIRE

TOOLS

· toothed pliers
· torch

MATERIALS

· wire

1. Hold the wire securely with pliers, straight up and down, and keep the tip of the wire in the hottest part of the flame, which is just past the inner bright blue cone.

2. When a ball forms, gently remove the wire from the flame, and quench it in water.

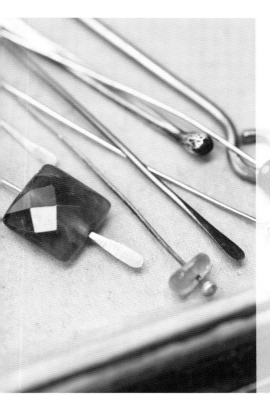

Head Pins Three Ways

TOOLS

- chain-nose pliers
- round-nose pliers
- flush cutters
- hammer
- bench block
- torch
- fine-grit foam sanding block

MATERIALS

- wire

A. Hammer the end flat.

B. Heat the end to form a bead.

C. Form a loop on the paddle end.

D. Center the loop over the wire.

PADDLE HEAD PIN

1. Flush cut a 3" (7.6 cm) length of wire, using an appropriate gauge for the project.

2. Working on the bench block, hammer a paddle at one end (see A).

BALL HEAD PIN

1. Flush cut a 3½" (8.9 cm) length of wire, using a gauge appropriate for the project.

2. Draw a bead on one end using a torch (see B).

3. Sand the beaded end with a fine-grit foam sanding block.

EYE HEAD PIN

1. Flush cut a 3½" (8.9 cm) length of wire, using an appropriate gauge for the project.

2. Hammer a slight paddle at one end.

3. Place the paddle end of the wire into round-nose pliers, a quarter of the way from the tips, and form a closed loop (see C).

4. Center the loop over the wire with a backward motion of the pliers (see D). Close the loop again if necessary.

WRAPPED LINK

TOOLS

- chain-nose pliers
- round-nose pliers
- flush cutters
- hammer
- bench block

MATERIALS

- wire
- bead

A. Bend the wire in the center.

B. Wrap wire around the pliers.

C. Wrap wire around the base.

D. Add a bead and make another loop.

1. Cut about 5" (12.7 cm) of wire. Beginning in the center, using chain-nose pliers, bend the wire to a 90-degree angle (see A).

2. Using round-nose pliers, bend the wire up and over the barrel of the pliers until it will go no further (see B).

3. Without removing the pliers, open them slightly, and spin them toward you. Close the pliers and continue wrapping the wire the rest of the way to make a loop.

4. Grasp the loop with the chain-nose pliers, and then use your fingers to wrap the wire around the base of the loop, turning the wire like a crank (see C).

5. Trim the end of the wire with flush cutters, and squeeze the end in with chain-nose pliers.

6. Add a bead to the wire, and finish the link by creating a loop on the other end of the wire, following the steps above (see D).

7. Slightly flatten loops if desired.

Wrapped Briolette Drop

TOOLS

- flush cutters
- chain-nose pliers
- round-nose pliers
- hammer
- bench block

MATERIALS

- wire
- top-drilled briolette bead

A. Add a bead.

B. Cross the wire ends.

C. Make loop and center it over the bead.

1. Flush cut 8"–10" (20.3–25.4 cm) of 24- or 26-gauge wire, depending on what will fit through your bead hole. Insert the wire into the briolette hole about one-third of the way down the wire (see A).

2. Cross both wires over the top of the briolette, squeezing the wire tightly to the bead (see B).

3. With round-nose pliers, wrap the shorter end of the wire over the barrel of the pliers to form a loop. Center the loop over the briolette (see C).

4. Grasp the loop with chain-nose pliers, and wrap the shorter wire around the base of the loop, making sure to pass it to one side of the longer wire, and then to the other side on the next wrap. Continue wrapping the wire over the top of the bead. Trim and squeeze the end of the wire when you are finished wrapping.

5. Wrap the longer wire in the same way, covering some of the wrapping that has already been done. Trim and tuck the end in by squeezing the wire.

6. Adjust the wrapping with the chain-nose pliers if necessary. Flatten the loop slightly with a hammer.

COIL CRIMP END

TOOLS

- flush cutters
- bailing pliers
- chain-nose pliers
- hammer
- bench block
- torch (optional)
- fine-grit foam sanding block (optional)

MATERIALS

- wire
- necklace material: leather cord, ribbon, rubber cord

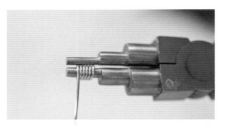

A. Wrap wire around the pliers.

B. Trim end.

C. Bend top loop perpendicular to wire.

D. Insert cord and squeeze bottom coil.

E. Flatten loop.

1. Flush cut 6"–8" (15.2–20.3 cm) of 20-gauge or heavier wire.

    Optional: Draw a bead on both ends of the wire. Clean the balled ends with a fine-grit foam sanding block.

2. Determine the diameter of the coil to be made. The material to be crimped will determine the diameter. For instance, a 1 mm round leather requires a smaller diameter coil than a 4 mm rubber cord.

3. Choose bailing pliers a bit larger than the size of coil needed. Wrap the wire around the barrel of the pliers to form a coil (see A). If you didn't draw a bead on your wire, snip the end with flush cutters (see B).

4. Using chain-nose pliers, bend the top loop on one end of the coil to be perpendicular and centered to the coil (see C).

5. Insert the necklace material (leather cord, rubber cord, sari silk, etc.) into the other end of the coil and close that end of the coil onto the material, squeezing tightly with chain-nose pliers (see D).

6. Slightly flatten the loop with a hammer (see E).

HOOK CLOSURES

TOOLS

- chain-nose pliers
- round-nose pliers
- extra-long round-nose pliers
- 5-7-10 mm bailing pliers
- flush cutters
- jewelry hammer
- dead-blow hammer
- bench block
- torch

MATERIALS

- wire

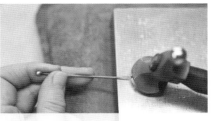

A. Flatten one end.

B. Make a loop on paddle end.

C. Make a hook on beaded end.

D. Turn up the hook.

E. Flatten with a hammer.

SINGLE BALL HOOK

1. Flush cut 3¼" (8.5 cm) of 14-gauge sterling wire. Use the torch and draw a bead on one end. Flatten the other end with a hammer to form a paddle (see A).

2. Using the back of the extra-long round-nose pliers, make a small loop on the paddle end (see B).

3. Use the largest barrel of the 5-7-10 mm bailing pliers to make a large hook at the beaded end (see C).

4. Turn the end of the hook up slightly using the extra-long round-nose pliers (see D).

5. Flatten the hook and loop with the jewelry hammer (see E).

6. Harden the hook using the dead-blow hammer.

A. Make loop at one end.

B. Bend bottom of hook.

C. Form small loop.

D. Wrap wire above small loop.

E. Turn up hook end.

DOUBLE BALL WRAPPED HOOK

1. Cut a 4" (10 cm) of 14-gauge wire and draw a bead at both ends using the torch.

2. Create the hook as described for the "Single Ball Hook" (see A).

3. Using chain-nose pliers, bend the wire at the bottom of the hook to form a 90-degree angle with the wire and the hook (see B).

4. Form the small loop with the back of the extra-long round-nose pliers (see C).

5. Grasp the small loop using chain-nose pliers, and form a messy wrap above the small loop (see D).

6. Turn the end of the hook up slightly using the extra-long round-nose pliers (see E).

7. Flatten the hook and loop with jewelry hammer.

8. Harden using the dead-blow hammer.

SIMPLE HOOK

1. Flush cut 3¼" (8.5 cm) of 14-gauge wire, and hammer a small paddle at both ends.

2. Using the back of the extra-long round-nose pliers, make a small loop at one end.

3. Using round-nose pliers and holding the wire so the small loop is pointing away from you, make a tiny loop at the other end.

4. Place the largest barrel of the 5-7-10 mm bailing pliers just under the tiny loop and create the hook.

5. Flatten the small loop and hook using a hammer.

6. Harden the hook with a dead-blow hammer.

WORKING WITH VINTAGE CLASPS

TOOLS

- flush cutters
- chain-nose pliers
- round-nose pliers

MATERIALS

- wire
- vintage rhinestone clasps
- beads

A. Add wire to clasp and make a loop.

B. Attach other end to clasp; close loop.

LINK CONNECTION

See "Wrapped Link" on page 40 for images showing the link process.

1. For each link cut 3"–4" (7.5 –10 cm) of 22- or 24-gauge wire. Beginning in the center of the wire and using chain-nose pliers, bend the wire to a 90-degree angle.

2. Using round-nose pliers, bend the wire up and over the barrel of the pliers until it will go no further.

3. Without removing the pliers, open them slightly and spin them toward you. Close the pliers, and continue wrapping the wire the rest of the way to make a small loop.

4. Connect the loop to the clasp. Grasp the loop with chain-nose pliers, and with your fingers wrap the wire around the base of the loop, turning the wire like a crank.

5. Trim the end of the wire with flush cutters, and squeeze in the end with the chain-nose pliers.

6. Add a bead to the wire and finish the link by creating a loop on the other end of the bead, following the same steps above.

7. Repeat steps for all the links to be connected to the clasp.

BEADED-LOOP CONNECTION

1. Cut 3"–4" (7.5–10 cm) of 26-gauge wire. Make a tiny loop about two-thirds of the way from one end of the wire and thread it onto the clasp. Grasp the loop with chain-nose pliers, close the loop, and wrap the wire one or two times around base of the loop (see A).

2. Thread seed beads, or other small beads, onto the wire.

3. Using your fingers, gently bend the wire with the beads into a rounded shape.

4. Insert the other end of the wire onto the clasp. Grasp the loop with the chain-nose pliers, close the loop, and wrap the wire one or two times around the base of the loop (see B).

STRIΠGIΠG BEADS AΠD USIΠG CRIMP TUBES

TOOLS

- bead stoppers
- crimp pliers or Magical Crimping Tool
- chain-nose pliers
- flush cutters

MATERIALS

- beading wire
- crimp tubes
- beads

A. Secure beads with stopper.

B. Crimp looks like a ravioli.

C. Squeeze crimp tube.

D. Secure crimp tube and trim wire.

1. String beads onto the beading wire and use a bead stopper to secure one end (see A).

2. String a crimp tube onto the other end, string the wire through the clasp or connector, and then back through the crimp tube.

3. Use the crimp tool to squeeze and flatten the crimp tube; if you use the Magical Crimping Tool, the crimp tube will now look like a tiny ravioli (see B). Rotate the crimp tool, and squeeze the tube again (see C). The tube will begin to look like a tiny, oval-shaped bead. Continue rotating the crimp tool and squeezing the tube to smooth the bead.

4. Squeeze the crimped tube with chain-nose pliers to completely secure; trim the wire (see D).

CUTTING AND FILING

TOOLS

- metal shears
- dead-blow hammer
- #2 metal file
- bench block
- fine-grit foam sanding block

MATERIALS

- metal

1. Use metal shears to cut sheet metal into the desired shape (see A).

2. If the metal edges are curled, gently hammer them flat with a dead-blow hammer (see B).

3. File edges using a #2 metal file, working only in a forward direction (see C).

4. Sand edges with a fine-grit foam sanding block (see D).

A. Cut metal.

B. Hammer curled edges flat.

C. File edges in forward motion.

D. Sand edges smooth.

DRILLING

TOOLS

- center punch
- jewelry hammer
- bench block
- titanium drill bits
- pliers
- flex-shaft or Dremel tool
- cylinder diamond bit

MATERIALS

- metal
- bit lubricant
- poster tack
- plastic container
- mother-of-pearl, glass, or stone object

A. Hammer a divot in metal.

B. Position bit in divot, and drill.

DRILLING METAL

1. Use the center punch and hammer to make a small divot for the desired hole (see A).

2. Dip the titanium bit into bit lubricant. Hold the metal to be drilled with pliers, and place the bit's tip into the divot. Turn on the flex-shaft or Dremel tool, gently press down through the metal, and then back up with a steady motion (see B).

DRILLING MOTHER-OF-PEARL, STONE, OR GLASS

1. Embed the object into the poster tack. Affix the poster tack to the bottom of a plastic container, and barely cover it with water.

2. Using the cylinder-shaped diamond bit in a flex-shaft or Dremel tool, hover over the area to be drilled, and slowly lower the bit onto the object.

3. Use a slow, steady speed and pressure to drill through the object. The object and bit should be covered by a very small amount of water to keep the bit cool.

setting eyelets

TOOLS

· flex-shaft or Dremel tool
· 1/16" (2 mm) titanium drill bit
· center punch
· jewelry hammer
· bench block
· pliers
· awl

MATERIALS

· metal or object
· 1/16" (2 mm) eyelets

A. Use an awl to insert eyelet.

B. Flatten eyelet with a hammer.

1. To drill a hole, see "Drilling Metal" on page 48.

2. If necessary, use the awl to ream the hole and enlarge it. Pick up an eyelet with the awl and insert the eyelet into the hole (see A).

3. Flip the piece over and using a center punch and hammer, insert the center-punch tip into the eyelet and gently hammer it halfway down (see B).

4. Using the ball end of the jewelry hammer, gently flatten the eyelet the rest of the way.

making a wire rivet

TOOLS

- center punch
- jewelry hammer
- bench block
- pliers
- ¹⁄₁₆" (2 mm) titanium drill bit
- flex-shaft or Dremel tool
- flush cutters
- bench vise

MATERIALS

- metal or object to be riveted
- 14-gauge wire

A. Drill holes in both objects.

B. Hammer wire end to flatten.

C. Hammer edges to form rounded shape.

D. Insert rivet, turn over, and cut wire.

E. Hammer the wire into rounded shape.

1. Drill a hole. For the rivet, flush-cut about 4" (10 cm) of 14-gauge wire, and place it in the vise so that about ⅛" (3 mm) sticks up from the vise surface. If metals or objects are to be layered, drill a hole in the top layer first, and use the hole to mark the hole for the second layer before drilling. Continue in the same manner for additional layers (see A).

2. Using the ball end of a jewelry hammer, gently hammer the top of the wire while pushing the wire upward with steady pressure beneath the vise (see B). Hammer slightly around the edges of the surface of the wire end.

3. Continue hammering gently until the wire surface mushrooms into a rounded rivet head (see C).

4. Insert the wire into the piece(s) to be riveted; the rounded head will act as a stopper. Flip the piece over and flush cut the wire to about ¹⁄₁₆" (2 mm) (see D).

5. Repeat steps 2 and 3 (see E).

LIVER-OF-SULFUR and HEaT PaTInas

TOOLS

- pliers
- torch
- fine-grit foam sanding block
- 0000 steel wool or manicure block

MATERIALS

- metal or wire
- liver-of-sulfur chunks
- protective gloves
- plastic containers
- micro wax (optional variation)

A. Liver-of-sulfur chunks

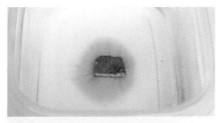

B. Dissolve liver-of-sulfur in hot water.

C. Soak the wire until blackened.

D. Rinse in clean water.

LIVER-OF-SULFUR PATINA

1. While liver-of-sulfur is not particularly toxic (see A), I always wear gloves when working with it. I also use it outdoors because its smell is very unpleasant.

2. Pour hot water (not boiling) into a plastic container, add a few chunks of liver-of-sulfur, and allow it to dissolve (see B). Fill a second container with cool rinse water.

3. Immerse the metal or wire into the liver-of-sulfur and allow it to blacken (see C).

4. Remove the wire or metal and place it in the rinse water (see D).

Rinse a second time, if desired, and dry with paper towels.

5. Polish with a fine-grit foam sanding block and/or steel wool or manicure block (see E). Any patina can be sealed with a micro wax product.

6. Dispose of the liver-of-sulfur mixture by allowing it to sit for a few days, and then dump it outside, flushing with clear water. Liver of sulfur dissipates with contact to air and light. Store the remaining liver-of-sulfur chunks in an airtight container away from light.

E. Polish the surfaces.

One should either be a work of art, or wear a work of art.

—OSCAR WILDE

CHAPTER 3

DESIGNING WITH
SHAPE, SIZE, and SPACE

SHAPE, SIZE, AND SPACE are some of the most obvious visual elements in jewelry making and, together, can be one of the most immediately recognizable. Using different shapes in a piece can convey excitement and interest, and working with found objects offers many opportunities for incorporating unusual shapes and interesting sizes. Beads and stones also come in an infinite variety of shapes: round, square, oval, bullet, teardrop, as well as nuggets, and freeform stones.

A piece of jewelry utilizing varying shapes and sizes, especially if the differences between shape and size are extreme, must be well designed with careful attention to placement and proportion. Differing shapes can be used to create tension and excitement in a piece. For instance, using a larger element here and there within a piece of jewelry draws the eye to those elements first. The contrast created between large and small elements is always interesting and can liven up an otherwise dull design. Asymmetrical designs are a great place to use multiple shapes and sizes, as long as the design is well thought-out.

Alternatively, using similar shapes and sizes, or echoing the same shape within a piece, offers a sense of harmony and rhythm. Repeating the same shape and size creates a balanced and uniform background for an outstanding and unique focal. If the focal is especially intricate, repetition in the rest of the piece offers a soothing counterpart.

Size refers to not only the size of the individual elements but also the piece of jewelry as a whole. Size comes into play when the designer considers who will be wearing the piece, how heavy the finished piece will be, and whether the piece will be wearable.

Space, or the area around and between objects, is another important design element in jewelry making. Positive space is the objects used, while negative space is the empty space around the objects. Negative space can have a huge impact on the way a piece is viewed, so make sure to consider it in your work. In a busy piece, negative space is especially important because it gives the eye a place to rest.

When jewelry is well designed, it doesn't have to be intricate for the visual impact of the shapes, sizes, and spacing to make the piece interesting.

MIDNIGHT ROSARIUM *Necklace*

TOOLS

- pliers; toothed, round-nose, extra-long round-nose, bailing, chain-nose
- torch
- metal shears
- metal file
- fine-grit foam sanding block
- center punch
- ball-peen hammer
- rawhide mallet or dead-blow hammer
- 1/16" (2 mm) titanium bit
- flex-shaft or Dremel tool
- bench block and bench pillow
- flush-cut wire snips
- craft knife

MATERIALS

- brass trim
- vintage paper
- mica
- dark annealed steel wire, 24-gauge
- sixteen 4 mm pyrite beads
- dark annealed steel wire, 20-gauge
- vintage crucifix
- two vintage religious medals
- six 22 mm onyx beads
- dark annealed steel wire, 18- or 20-gauge (for clasp)

A. Close-up of rosary and religious medal attachment

INSTRUCTIONS

1. Anneal a small amount of vintage brass trim. Cut the trim with metal shears to the desired size, file the edges, and then sand the edges with a sanding block.

2. Using a center punch, make four indentations in the corners of the brass trim in preparation for drilling. Drill the holes in the metal.

3. With a craft knife, cut a stack of paper the same dimensions as the brass trim. Cut mica to fit as well.

4. For the focal, layer the mica, paper, mica, and brass trim; clamp down. Using the holes in the metal as a guide, drill through all the layers.

5. Using 24-gauge wire and pyrite beads, wrap two links and attach them to the lower corners of the focal. Using 20-gauge wire, wrap another pyrite link, attach one end to the lower loops of both previous links, and attach the other end to the crucifix; close the link. For an alternate method, attach the crucifix using a jump ring. Using 20-gauge wire, wrap two more pyrite links and attach them end to end, connecting them to the same loop as the crucifix. Before closing the bottom loop, add a small religious medal (see A).

6. Using 20-gauge wire and pyrite beads, wrap and connect two links at the top of the focal.

7. Use 20-gauge wire to wrap the remaining six onyx and eight pyrite beads to form the rest of the links. Join the links, alternating the onyx and pyrite beads. For the last pyrite link that attaches to the hook, use extra-long round-nose pliers on one end of the link. This will form the eye for the hook-and-eye closure.

8. Use 18- or 20-gauge wire and bailing pliers to make a hook for the clasp.

9. Wrap and connect three more pyrite links, attaching the first link at the base of the hook, and attaching a religious medal to the last link (see B).

B. Close-up of clasp and medal attachment

JOURNAL Notes

One of the things I love most about this piece is the juxtaposition of a little bit of sparkle with a little bit of boho grunge. I intentionally used large, faceted midnight-black onyx with small cut pyrite to contrast with the mellow color of the steel wire. To accent the shape and size of the onyx beads, I paired them with the much smaller pyrite. This brings attention first to the focal, then to the onyx, and leads the eye up the piece. The neutral color scheme makes this a very versatile necklace for everyday wear.

This type of focal is one of my favorite ways to add interest to a piece of jewelry. The sandwiched vintage pages, mica, and metal make for a very special mini book. The shape immediately draws the viewer's eye and prompts further investigation. On closer look, the viewer discovers the delightful stack of text. Who doesn't love a good book?

DESIGN Tips

· I found my vintage brass trim at an antique store. If you don't have a source for vintage brass trim, try using new filigree. Metal filigree can be found online, and there are so many lovely shapes and sizes that it is hard to choose!

· Pages from any vintage book can be used for the focal. Also try using an interesting found object, such as a vintage locket watch fob, in place of the crucifix.

soul mates Earrings

TOOLS

- metal shears
- fine-grit foam sanding block
- metal file
- center punch
- jewelry hammer
- bench block and bench pillow
- pliers; round-nose, chain-nose, stepped-bailing
- $\frac{1}{16}$" (2 mm) titanium bit, or hand drill
- flex-shaft or Dremel tool
- awl
- rawhide mallet or dead-blow hammer
- flush cut wire snips
- butane torch

MATERIALS

- two gem tintypes
- spray acrylic sealer
- metal trim or filigree
- $\frac{1}{16}$" (2 mm) short eyelets
- sterling silver wire, 22-gauge
- rhinestone chain
- sterling silver wire, 20-gauge
- sterling silver wire, 24- or 26-gauge
- two 6–8 mm top-drilled briolette beads
- two 8 mm metal beads
- two small rhinestone dangles
- sterling silver wire, 14-gauge

INSTRUCTIONS

1. Spray the tintypes with acrylic sealer three times, allowing the sealer to dry between each coat.

2. Cut the tintypes to the desired shape using the metal shears. Lightly sand the edges with a sanding block, and spray a final coat of sealer on both sides.

3. Cut metal trim or filigree to fit the bottom of the tintypes; file and sand the edges.

4. Drill $\frac{1}{16}$" (2 mm) holes on each side of the metal trim, using the center punch to mark for drilling. Fit the trim on the bottom of tintypes, and mark the tintype where holes will be drilled.

5. Drill holes in the tintypes, and then rivet the metal trim to the tintypes (See A).

6. Use the center punch to mark the top of each tintype for drilling. Drill the holes and set with eyelets.

7. Using 22-gauge wire and the small tip of the stepped-bailing pliers, make four coil-crimp ends. Cut two rhinestone chains, each long enough to hang from the top of the tintype to below the lower edge. Attach a crimp end to each end of the chains.

A. Rivet the metal to the tintype.

8. Using 24- or 26-gauge wire, wrap two briolette beads. Attach the wrapped briolettes to the coil crimp at one end of each rhinestone chain.

9. Using 22-gauge wire, make two wrapped links using the metal beads. Before closing one end, attach one rhinestone chain, one tintype, and one small rhinestone dangle in that order, to each link.

10. Using 20-gauge wire, make two ear wires. Ball one end and flatten it before shaping the ear wires. Attach to the earrings and close the ear wires securely.

DESIGN Tips

- A short length of metal chain can be used in place of the rhinestone chain, which would eliminate the need for the wrapped crimp ends.

- If you don't have small rhinestone dangles, improvise by making your own from a small faceted bead and a homemade headpin.

- If you would rather not use rivets to connect the metal trim to the tintype, use $1/16$" (2 mm) eyelets or micro bolts instead. Escutcheon pins are also a great alternative to rivets. These pins are really tiny nails, with a rounded head, so half the work of rivet making is already done. Make sure to purchase escutcheon pins that are all-brass and not plated.

JOURNAL Notes

Antique tintypes are a cherished part of photographic history, and gem types are the charming little crown jewels of that era. Photographers used a multiplying camera, which produced many images on a single plate. The resulting postage-stamp size gems are the perfect size for use in jewelry making.

Rather than leave the tintypes in their original shape, I have cut and filed them, and set them with some vintage metal trim. The shape makes them immediately more eye-catching. I rarely find two gem types of the same subject, so I paired this man and woman to make them eternal soul mates. The dissimilarity makes them more interesting, as does the addition of a little color and sparkle with the rhinestones and facets.

GO BIG, TEXAS-STYLE Necklace

TOOLS

- pliers; round-nose, chain-nose
- jewelry hammer
- rawhide mallet or dead-blow hammer
- bench block and bench pillow
- flush cut wire snips
- compound flush cutters such as Power Max
- metal file
- fine-grit foam sanding block
- awl
- flex-shaft, Dremel tool, or hand drill
- $\frac{1}{16}$" (2 mm) titanium bit

MATERIALS

- sterling silver wire, 22-gauge
- five vintage rhinestone brooches; 1 large, 2 medium, 2 small
- one vintage watch fob swivel clasp
- one small vintage rhinestone button
- large vintage religious medal
- nine 20 mm gemstone beads
- one vintage rhinestone buckle or clasp

DESIGN Tips

- When you are making connections between links and elements, lay the piece out periodically to make sure everything lies properly.

- If you don't have a vintage religious medal for the focal, or don't want to use a religious piece, many other found objects will work. Just make sure that whatever you choose is in proportion to the rest of the design.

- For this necklace, I used rock crystal gemstones. Other stones will work as long as the proportion, size, and color go with the brooches you choose.

- I used a vintage rhinestone buckle to close this necklace, but you could easily use a large rhinestone clasp, or create a hook-and-eye closure.

A. Close-up of swivel attachment

C. Close-up of buckle clasp

INSTRUCTIONS

1. Prepare the brooches by removing the pin backs with flush cutters; file and sand.

2. Where the brooches will be connected to the necklace, use an awl to remove any rhinestones to prepare for drilling.

3. Carefully drill holes where the rhinestones were removed. Drill slowly as many vintage pieces are soft pot metal.

4. Flush cut 6" (15 cm) of wire, and make a wire-wrapped link, connecting one end to the bottom of the largest brooch before closing the wrap. At the other end, add the watch fob swivel clasp and the small rhinestone button before closing the wrap.

5. Attach the vintage religious medal to the fob swivel clasp (see A).

6. Build the rest of the piece from the focal upward, adding wire wrapped links with stones, and connecting the remaining brooches (see B).

7. Before closing the last wire wrapped link, make the loop big enough to connect a vintage buckle as a clasp (see C).

B. Connect remaining brooches with wrapped links.

JOURNAL Notes

In Texas, everything really is bigger—and blingier! I was lucky enough to find a bunch of similar rhinestone brooches for sale at one of my teaching venues and snapped them up quickly. I could not resist putting them all in the same piece; I found them together and thought they needed to stay together. The shapes and sizes just happened to work perfectly for a large statement necklace.

Proportion is important in a large piece. To keep it right, I used huge rock crystal gemstone beads between each brooch. The stones' clear color doesn't distract from the rhinestone pieces, and they don't add any more sparkle, but rather a low-level shine that is just right. Size, proportion, and shape are important to good design when you are using such large elements.

This piece is a stunner, fit for a night out with your favorite little black dress. But in Texas we would just as soon wear our bling with boots and a denim shirt. Either way, big and bold is a great design strategy when it is done right.

CREATION *Necklace*

TOOLS

- pliers; round-nose, extra-long round-nose, chain-nose
- ball-peen hammer
- rawhide mallet or dead-blow hammer
- bench block and bench pillow
- flush cut wire snips
- metal shears
- metal file
- bead crimping pliers
- torch

MATERIALS

- steel wire, 26-gauge
- steel wire, 24-gauge
- steel wire, 20-gauge
- steel wire, 18- or 16-gauge (for clasp)
- beading wire, medium weight
- brass trim
- ammonite fossil, approximately 35 mm x 40 mm
- three 14 mm faceted smoky quartz
- two 24 mm faceted agate beads
- two 12 mm metal beads
- one 20 mm center-drilled jasper flower bead
- approximately 7" (18 cm) of 4 mm heishi beads
- sterling silver crimp tubes, 2 mm x 2 mm

JOURNAL Notes

It seems I have two jewelry-making personae, with some of my pieces falling somewhere between the two. One personality is girly, sparkly, and edgy bling—industrial romance. And one personality is grungy, heavy metal, dark, and a little creepy—boho grunge. This piece falls into the second category. Fossils have been a favorite found object of mine since I was a kid. The shapes, sizes, and textures are so varied and interesting, not to mention their history. One day I picked up this ammonite in one hand and the vintage brass trim in the other; it was cosmic chemistry!

The faceted stones add the perfect touch of sparkle to this piece. It is a grungy look, so I didn't want to go overboard. Keeping to one color scheme complements the focal and keeps the attention where it belongs. The wirework makes the piece completely unique and adds an industrial touch. Notice how space comes into play with the wire elements—it is a bit of relief for the eye from the chunky beads and unique fossil, while still being interesting. The smooth strand of heishi beads also provides a resting place for the eye. I added the jasper flower bead to balance out the run of faceted smoky quartz.

INSTRUCTIONS

1. Use metal shears to cut a piece of brass trim to fit around the outside of the fossil for a bezel (see A). Solder the ends together using either the torch method or the soldering iron method. (Soldering instructions can be found online.)

2. For the wire part of the focal, form a framework by creating a wrapped loop in the center of a 12" (30.5 cm) piece of 24-gauge wire. Before closing, thread the focal onto the loop. Create a spiral at each end of the wire frame, ending about 1" (2.5 cm) above the loop. Just above the loop, begin wrapping with 26-gauge steel

A. Focal with a brass bezel

wire by securing the wire to one side of the frame, and then crossing over and wrapping around the other side. Continue wrapping until the framework is completed (see B).

3. Using 20-gauge wire, create a long wrapped link using three smoky quartz beads. Before closing, attach one end to the focal.

4. With 20-gauge wire, make wrapped links using one of the agate beads and one metal bead; attach these above the smoky quartz as shown in the photo, opposite.

5. For the other side of the necklace, use 18-gauge wire to make a loosely wrapped link with one loop being larger than the other. Attach the link to the focal before closing.

6. Use approximately 3" (7.5 cm) of 18-gauge wire to make a hook clasp.

7. Use 20-gauge wire to make wrapped links using the remaining agate and metal beads, and then attach them above the hook clasp.

8. Using 5" (12.5 cm) of 20-gauge wire, make a paddle-head pin, thread the jasper flower bead onto the pin, and wrap the top; attach it to the hook clasp.

9. Thread the heishi beads onto a medium beading wire, and attach each end to the necklace using crimp tubes.

DESIGN Tips

- Any kind of wire can be used for this project, but I love the boho look of steel wire.

- Paddle the ends of your wire when creating wrapped loops for more emphasis on detail.

- If you don't have this type of vintage brass trim, there are a few alternatives. You can wrap your fossil with copper tape used for stain-glass making, cover the tape with lead-free solder (using a soldering iron), and add a bail or jump ring. Or try your hand at a wire wrapped bezel; you can find tutorials online.

B. Wrap wire to form a framework.

LeatHer and RHinestones
Cuff Bracelet

TOOLS

- pliers; toothed, round-nose, chain-nose
- jewelry hammer
- rawhide mallet or dead-blow hammer
- bench block and bench pillow
- flush cut wire snips
- metal shears
- metal file
- fine-grit foam sanding block
- manicure block
- flex-shaft, Dremel tool, or hand drill
- $\frac{1}{16}$" (2 mm) titanium bit
- torch
- Japanese screw punch
- needles; cotton darning no. 5, tapestry no. 24
- scissors

MATERIALS

- bronze wire, 20-gauge
- leather scrap
- four brass trim, filigree, or textured metal
- three vintage rhinestone buttons, shank style; one large, two medium
- jewelry glue
- upholstery or beading thread

INSTRUCTIONS

1. Cut the leather scrap to 6¾" x 1¼" (17 x 3 cm), or wide enough to leave a narrow border on either side of the buttons when attached.

2. Anneal the metal trim, and use the shears to cut two pieces 2" (5 cm) long, and the same width as the leather strip; file and sand the rough edges.

3. Anneal the metal again, and fold in half. Use the bench block to help fold the metal almost all the way in half.

4. Cut two 9" (23 cm) pieces of wire and anneal. Insert the wire into the fold of the metal pieces. Insert the leather into the folded metal, and press the metal sides together with pliers. Use the dead-blow hammer or rawhide mallet to secure the leather in place.

5. Using pliers, fold the wire at one end, crossing it in the center. Bend one wire perpendicular to the metal end. Fold the other wire at a 90-degree angle from the first wire. Grasp the wire with pliers, and wrap once or twice around the base of the perpendicular wire. Wrap the perpendicular wire into a loop, wrapping a few times over the first wire (see A).

B. Close-up of back

6. At the other end of the bracelet, repeat the steps to attach the metal trim and wire. Instead of making a loop, make a small hook. If necessary, secure the metal ends with small amount of jewelry glue, and clamp overnight. Buff all metal and wire with the manicure block.

7. On the leather, mark where the buttons will be attached, and make holes with a screw punch. With a darning needle, make a small hole on either side of the punched holes.

8. Fit the button shanks into the holes, and stitch using a tapestry needle and upholstery thread. Stitch only into the small holes made with darning needle. Stitch through the shank and into the leather a few times, securing the button tightly to the leather (see B and C).

A. Detail of wire clasp

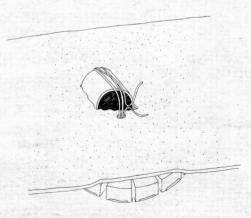

C. Detail of stitching on back

JOURNAL Notes

This bracelet is the quintessential mix of biker and bling. The sparkling buttons and textured metal give it a very Victorian feel, while the leather exudes a modern vibe. This would be the perfect way to use some sentimental buttons from your grandmother's collection.

The spacing and size of the buttons is important in this piece. I almost went with the large center button, two medium-size buttons, and two small ones at each end. Five would have been fine—just more bling—but I decided on a simpler look, and used only three buttons. When I first designed this bracelet I had the large oval button turned the other way. I quickly realized that it looked much better lengthwise. I tried several different buttons for accents and finally landed on the two I used. One of them is purposely less shiny, with a more worn look—it helps add to the boho feeling of bringing disparate objects together.

DESIGN Tips

- Once leather is pierced, the hole is permanent. It is best to make pilot holes, so when you start stitching you always go through the same hole. I used a darning needle to make my holes for stitching, but any large needle will do. I used a tapestry needle for the actual stitching. It has a blunt tip so there is no danger of accidentally puncturing the leather.

- If you don't want this much sparkle, try using mother-of-pearl, or antique metal buttons. If you use buttons without a shank, create pilot holes with the darning needle so you can easily stitch through the leather.

- Leather comes in all kinds of finishes and colors. You should be able to find a package of scraps at your local craft store.

- I used brass trim for my metal ends, but new filigree, or textured metal would be lovely as well. Just make sure to secure it tightly to the leather. If necessary, don't hesitate to use a couple of drops of glue, as insurance.

These gems have life in them: their colors speak, say what words fail of.

—GEORGE ELIOT

CHAPTER 4

DESIGNING WITH
TEXTURE and COLOR

WHETHER IT IS THE HARD, smooth surface of polished metal or the soft surface of a fabric focal, texture is a part of all jewelry. There are two types of texture used in jewelry making—physical and visual. Physical textures are the facets, shapes, and surfaces you can feel. Visual texture is seen in things such as color, contrast, patina, shine, and sparkle. In a good design, physical and visual textures merge to create a perfect fusion.

Color, contrast, and sparkle allow the designer to create visual texture. Color is a strong visual draw while contrast adds the play of light: light, dark, and brightness. Sparkle adds a burst of light for drama. When designing, think of other forms of contrast as well: old and new, smooth and rough, hard and soft, or grungy and romantic. One of my favorite ways to use contrast is to combine edgy, grungy, metal elements with softer, more romantic, and sparkly pieces. Unexpected combinations add excitement to found-object jewelry.

Color is one of the most thrilling elements in your work, and is vital to communicate the mood of your jewelry. A block (or strand) of color will attract the eye. Bright or strong colors make a bold statement; soft or dull colors impart a more subtle feeling. Harmonizing colors are pleasing, while clashing colors are upsetting to the eye. Purchase a color wheel—it will make understanding color relationships and combinations much easier. I suggest making a color palette for your designs by cutting color snippets from a magazine and pasting them into your jewelry journal. A palette helps you select colors that harmonize well together. A common mistake is combining too many colors into the mix, which detracts from an otherwise great design. I usually limit myself to one or two colors, and frequently work in monochromatic color schemes. Since I often work with found objects, I find a limited palette helps my stones and objects sing.

An achromatic combination is a colorless scheme that combines blacks, whites, and grays. These are neutral colors, along with the metal colors of brass, bronze, silver, copper, and gold. An achromatic scheme is good if you are unsure color-wise, and it is easy to add an accent color.

everyday BOHO Earrings

TOOLS

- pliers; toothed, round-nose, bailing, chain-nose
- jewelry hammer
- rawhide mallet or dead-blow hammer
- bench block and bench pillow
- flush cut wire snips
- fine-grit foam sanding block
- butane torch

MATERIALS

- sterling silver wire, 20-gauge
- sterling silver wire, 22-gauge
- sterling silver wire, 24- or 26-gauge
- two 10 mm top-drilled briolette beads or center-drilled beads
- forty 4 mm gemstone beads

DESIGN Tips

- These hoops can be made in any size by simply threading more of the smaller beads onto a longer piece of wire. The shape can be easily adjusted as well.

- The facets of the beads give these hoops physical texture while the sparkle adds visual texture. I used pyrite for the silver-toned pair, and glass crystals with a hematite dangle for the blue pair. Instead of using just one size, shape, or color, try using a variety of beads on each hoop for even more texture.

- I used stones as my dangles, but nearly anything will work. A small charm, medal, or other trinket would be beautiful.

INSTRUCTIONS

1.   Prepare a dangle. For a briolette, wrap a loop at the top using 24- or 26-gauge wire (use the gauge that fits through the bead hole). For a center-drilled bead, draw a bead on one end of a 3" (7.5 cm) length of 24-gauge wire. Thread the bead onto the wire, and wrap a loop at the top. Set the dangle aside.

2.   Thread 4 mm beads onto 6" (15 cm) of 22-gauge wire, adding the dangle at the halfway point (see A).

3.   Shape the wire into a hoop, and wrap a loop at the top.

4.   Make ear wires using 20-gauge wire. As an option, ball one end before shaping the ear wires. Attach the earrings, and close ear wires securely.

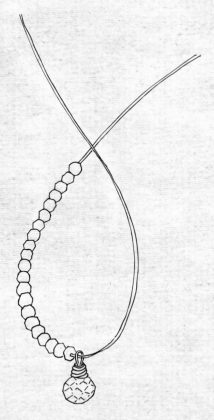

A. Thread beads onto the wire.

JOURNAL *Note*

These hoops are proof that sometimes less is more. The simple design is made striking by using sparkle as visual texture. I love the fact that these can be dressed up or down. The boho elegance goes equally as well with a little black dress or with jeans— I wear them for everyday.

SHIELD PRAYER-KEEPER *Necklace*

TOOLS

- pliers; toothed, round-nose, chain-nose
- crimp tool
- jewelry hammer
- rawhide mallet or dead-blow hammer
- bench block and bench pillow
- flush cut wire snips
- compound flush cutters
- metal file
- fine-grit foam sanding block
- awl
- flex-shaft or Dremel tool
- 1/16" (2 mm) titanium bit
- hand drill
- cylinder-shaped diamond bit
- plastic container
- poster tack

MATERIALS

- sterling silver wire, 22-gauge
- medium weight beading wire
- vintage mother-of-pearl bird
- vintage bone needle case (or similar object)
- vintage rhinestone brooch or dress clip
- one 8 mm crystal rondelle
- two 6 mm vintage crystal spacer beads
- two 5 mm round faceted carnelian beads
- two 10 mm round mother-of-pearl beads
- one 30 mm carnelian faceted tube bead
- one 7 mm round faceted vintage crystal bead
- two 7 mm round faceted carnelian beads
- five 5 mm round mother-of-pearl beads
- one 16" (40.5 m) strand 4 mm faceted hessonite garnet beads
- 2 mm sterling crimp tubes
- antique watch fob
- vintage rhinestone clasp
- vintage watch chain with swivel clasp
- seven 8 mm round, flat faceted hessonite garnet bead

A. Bird connected to needle case

B. Needle case connection

C. Close-up of clasp

INSTRUCTIONS

1. Embed the mother-of-pearl piece into poster tack, and adhere it firmly to the bottom of the plastic container; just cover with water. Using a diamond bit, drill a hole in the mother-of-pearl.

2. Prepare the needle case by carefully drilling a hole in each end—if necessary, use a hand drill.

3. Prepare the brooch by removing the back with compound flush cutters; file and sand. With an awl, remove the rhinestones in the corners. Drill holes where the rhinestones were removed.

4. For the connection between the bird and needle case, draw a bead on 4" (10 cm) of 22-gauge wire. Thread the wire through the bottom of the case, using the balled end as a stopper. Thread a crystal stopper, crystal rondelle, and another crystal stopper onto the wire, and wrap a loop to connect the bird piece (see A).

5. Do the same for the connection between the needle case and brooch, adding 5 mm carnelian beads in place of the crystals (see B).

6. Make two wrapped-link connections at the top of the brooch, using the 10 mm mother-of-pearl beads.

7. Prepare a vintage rhinestone clasp by creating and attaching four wire-wrapped links (two for each side) using the 5 mm mother-of-pearl beads and 22-gauge wire (see C).

8. For each side of the necklace, string 8" (20.5 cm) of the 4 mm hessonite garnet beads onto 12" (30.5 cm) of beading wire. Attach one end of each length to the mother-of-pearl links attached to the focal and the other end of each length to the links attached to the clasp (see D). Secure the beading wire using the 2 mm crimp tubes and a crimp tool.

9. Create wrapped links with the gemstones and 22-gauge wire, and attach the links to the clasp and focal on each side of the necklace, adding the watch-fob chain and swivel clasp on both sides as shown.

10. Make wrapped links using the round, flat hessonite garnet beads and 22-gauge wire. Attach the links to the back of the necklace at the clasp, adding a few links of watch-fob chain, and the fob at the end.

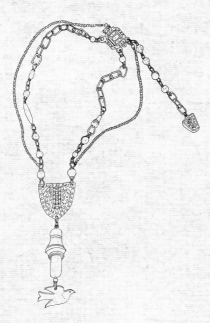

D. Attach strung beads to focal and clasp.

DESIGN Tips

- You probably won't find the same objects that I used in this piece. When you are out shopping, keep your eyes open for lots of interesting objects. They will work, as long as you keep them in proportion and stay within your color scheme.

- The antique bone needle case enables the wearer to personalize this piece by opening and tucking a written prayer or intention inside. I love pieces that contain a little element of surprise.

- Rhinestones create an intense sparkle and contrast. If you use them sparingly, think about sprinkling them throughout the piece to maintain balance.

JOURNAL Notes

This piece is loaded with texture and interesting objects. The focal is made up of three highly textured elements: a sparkling rhinestone dress clip, a carved bone needle case, and a glowing mother-of-pearl bird. The rhinestone clip is a great example of both physical and visual texture combined. The nubby rhinestones are physical while the sparkle is visual. More physical texture is created in the combination of strung beads, chain, and wrapped bead links. Visual texture is found in the color and shine of the faceted beads as well as the duller patina of the vintage watch chain.

This piece has a lot going on so I wanted to stick with a muted, monochromatic color scheme. This helps the found objects to stand out and not become overwhelming. This piece would have a whole different look if I had used loud, saturated colors for the gemstones. A monochromatic scheme uses any tint, tone, or shade of the same color. While this scheme may not be as vibrant as some others, it lends a calm, elegant effect. A monochromatic scheme is easy to design with, easy to look at, and gives your work a pleasing, balanced look.

HIPPIE HOOP Earrings

TOOLS

- pliers; round-nose, extra-long round-nose, chain-nose
- jewelry hammer
- rawhide mallet or dead-blow hammer
- bench block and bench pillow
- flush cut wire snips
- fine-grit foam sanding block
- butane torch
- hoop mandrel
- alligator clips

MATERIALS

- sterling silver, bronze, or copper wire, 14-gauge
- sterling silver wire, 20-gauge
- sterling silver wire, 22-gauge (optional, for dangle)
- sterling silver, bronze, or copper wire, 24- or 26-gauge
- two 7 mm round, center-drilled beads (optional, for dangle)
- seven strips recycled sari silk
- seed beads and small gemstone beads

INSTRUCTIONS

1. Prepare the dangle. Draw a bead on one end of a 3" (7.5 cm) piece of 24-gauge wire. Thread on a bead and wrap a loop at the top; set the dangle aside.

2. Anneal the 14-gauge wire. Bend a loop at each end using the back of the round-nose pliers; flatten the ends of the loops (see A). Form the wire into hoops using the hoop mandrel. Harden the hoops on the bench block with a rawhide mallet or dead-blow hammer.

3. Wrap the hoops with sari silk, using alligator clips to hold it in place.

4. Using 24- or 26-gauge wire, begin at the base of one loop, wrap the wire several times to secure, and then overwrap the sari silk, adding seed beads as you wrap. Finish wrapping the wire at the base of the opposite loop, wrapping several times to secure. Repeat for the other hoop.

5. Using chain-nose pliers, turn loops up (see B).

6. Using 1¼" (3 cm) of 20-gauge wire, make the ear wires. Attach the wires to the earrings, and close the connecting loop securely.

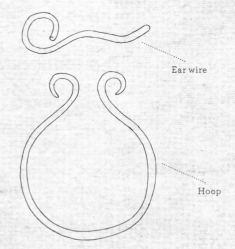

Ear wire

Hoop

B. Close-up of loops

A. Bend hoop and ear wires.

JOURNAL Note

I can't seem to get enough of hoops and these are a texture-laden version. Any color of silk and beads can be used to customize these for the wearer. They can be simple or loaded with beads and trinkets.

DESIGN Tips

- These hoops can be made in any size by adjusting the length of wire and sari silk used. Be mindful of weight when adding beads and embellishments. These earrings can quickly become uncomfortably heavy.

- Any lightweight fabric can be used to overwrap the wire hoop. For the smaller pair, I even added a bit of vintage tatting. The vintage black-glass-and-rhinestone montees were originally meant to be stitched onto clothing. They make a nice addition to these hoops.

steadfast heart sha   ill,
Thou, O Lord, art   ill:
y friendly crook shal   id,
And guide me through th   sh.

PSALM 34.

HROUGH all the changing s   e,
In trouble and in joy,
e praises of my God shall stil
My heart and tongue employ.
f His deliverance I will boast,
Till all that are distrest
om my example comfort take,
And charm their griefs to rest.
magnify the Lord with me,
With me exalt His Name!
en in distress on Him I called,
He to my rescue came.
e hosts of God encamp aroun
The dwellings of the just;
Deliverance He affords to all
Who on His succor trust.
O make but trial of His Love:
Experience will decide
How blest are they, and only
Who in His truth confide.

6 Fear Him, ye saints, and y
Have nothing else to fear
Make you His service you
He'll make your wants

Nahum Ta

87
1 HOW are Thy servants
How sure is their de
Eternal Wisdom is their
Their help Omnipotenc

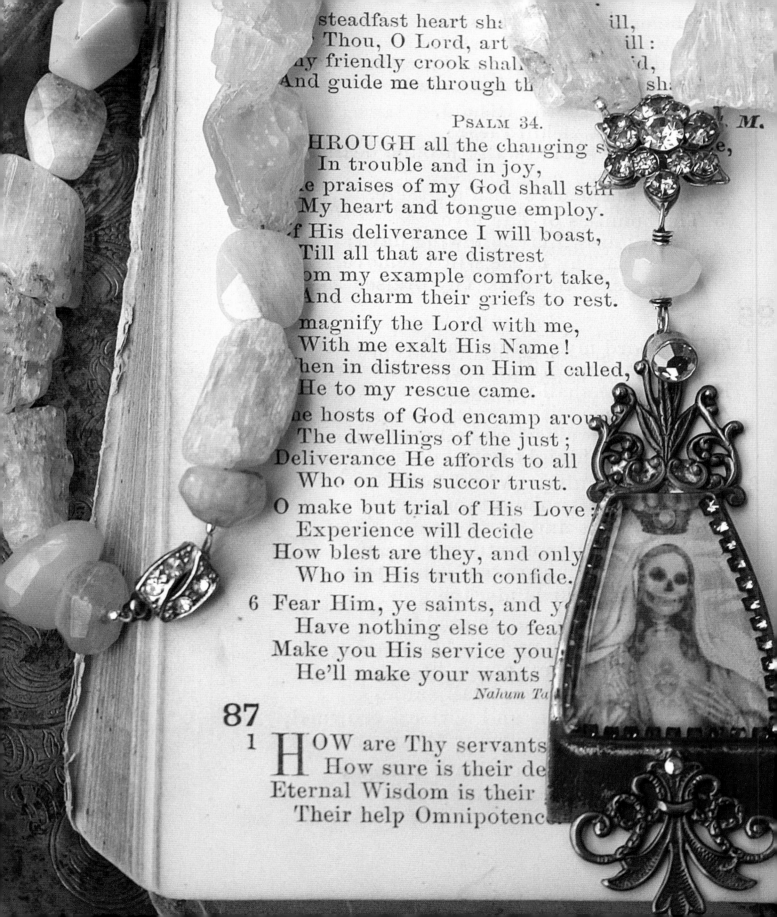

DIA DE LOS MUERTOS *Necklace*

TOOLS

- pliers; round-nose, chain-nose
- crimp tool
- jewelry hammer
- rawhide mallet or dead-blow hammer
- bench block and bench pillow
- flush cut wire snips
- Power Max flush cutters
- metal file
- fine-grit foam sanding block
- small paintbrush
- scissors

MATERIALS

- sterling silver wire, 22-gauge
- medium-weight beading wire
- image to fit inside bezel
- bezel for focal
- soft gel medium, gloss
- small rhinestone chain
- two-part resin such as ICE Resin
- small vintage rhinestone earring
- five 10–15 mm faceted green chalcedony beads
- 7 mm vintage rhinestone dangle
- one 6 mm jump ring
- thirteen 25–30 mm kunzite gemstone beads
- two 12 mm faceted aquamarine nugget beads
- three 15 mm faceted flat aquamarine beads
- one 15 mm faceted amazonite bead
- one 11 mm faceted rondelle aquamarine
- one 9 mm faceted square moss aquamarine bead
- 2 mm sterling crimp tubes
- vintage rhinestone clasp

JOURNAL Notes

I love taking photographs and like to use the images in my work but fell in love with this image, created by artist Robin Nowak. The soft colors and interesting concept appealed to me. When designing around an image, it's best to try to repeat a color or two from the image to create a harmonious and intentional look. Don't try to use every color from your focal as it can cause confusion. Referring to my color wheel, I decided to use a split complementary color scheme.

A split complementary scheme uses one color and both colors on either side of that color's complement. This split complementary scheme allows for contrast without the high impact of a straight complementary scheme. My split complementary palette includes tints, tones, and shades of a red/blue-green/yellow-green combination. This soft palette makes for a very quiet effect, which is what I was aiming for. I created this necklace to be worn with my "Spirits Necklace" (page 139) and I needed a calming design to go with the chaotic charm of that piece.

A. Detail of bezel focal

INSTRUCTIONS

1. For the focal, trim the image to fit the bezel, and coat both sides with gel medium three times, allowing the medium to dry between coats.

2. Affix the image inside the bezel using the gel medium. Trim the rhinestone chain to fit around the inside of the bezel; adhere with gel medium. Mix and pour resin according to the package instructions, and allow the resin to set for at least twenty-four hours (see A).

3. Cut off the earring back and file smooth. Make a wrapped link using one of the smaller chalcedony beads, and attach the link to the earring bottom and the top of the bezel, making sure to add the dangle using a jump ring, before closing the bottom loop (see B).

4. String gemstone beads onto about 8" (20.5 cm) of beading wire similar to the necklace shown; attach with crimp tubes on either side of the earring and to either side of the clasp (see C). To make the necklace longer or shorter, adjust the length of beading wire and amount of beads.

B. Close-up of rhinestone-earring connector

C. Close-up of clasp

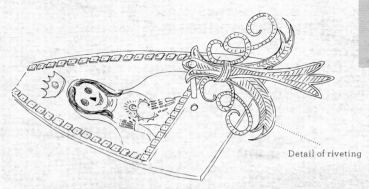

Detail of riveting

Side view of bezel

FOX and GRAPES *Necklace*

TOOLS

- pliers; round-nose, chain-nose, extra-long round-nose
- crimp tool
- jewelry hammer
- rawhide mallet or dead-blow hammer
- bench block and bench pillow
- flush cut wire snips
- compound flush cutters such as Power Max
- metal file
- fine-grit foam sanding block
- small paintbrush
- scissors

MATERIALS

- sterling silver wire, 22-gauge
- sterling silver wire, 24-gauge
- sterling silver wire, 26-gauge
- image to fit inside bezel
- purchased bezel for accent
- soft gel medium, gloss
- two-part resin such as ICE Resin
- vintage metal brooch
- 40 mm handmade lamp-work glass dangle
- sixteen 15–17 mm emerald gemstone beads
- two 9 mm vintage rhinestone dangles
- one 18 mm faceted top-drilled amethyst briolette
- vintage clasp
- seed beads
- two 7 mm rhinestone rondelles
- one 20 mm handmade lamp-work round bead
- vintage watch fob
- one 8 mm jump ring (optional)

A. Close-up of focal

B. Close-up of clasp

INSTRUCTIONS

1. For the bezel accent, trim the image to fit the bezel and coat both sides with gel medium three times, allowing to dry between coats. Affix the image inside the bezel using the gel medium. Mix and pour the resin according to the package instructions, and allow the resin to set for at least twenty-four hours.

2. Prepare the focal by removing the back; file smooth.

3. With 7" (18 cm) of 22-gauge wire, make a large loop using the back of the extra-long round-nose pliers, and attach the lamp-work glass dangle before closing the loop. Thread an emerald bead onto the wire, and then make another large loop, add a vintage rhinestone dangle, and attach this assemblage to the bottom of the focal before closing the loop (see A).

4. Prepare an amethyst drop by wrapping a briolette bead with 24-gauge wire, and make a loop at the top; set aside.

5. Prepare the clasp by attaching a loop on each side made from 26-gauge wire threaded with seed beads (see B); set aside.

6. On one side of the focal, make and connect three wire-wrapped links using 22-gauge wire and emerald stones. Attach one end of the links to the resin-bezel accent piece, including the amethyst drop (or attach it with a jump ring) (see C). Wrap and attach three more emerald links above the bezel, and end by attaching the last link to the clasp.

7. Do the same on the opposite side using two wrapped emerald links, attaching one to the focal.

8. Make a wrapped link using 22-gauge wire, two rhinestone rondelles, and the large round, lamp-work glass bead. Attach this link above the two emerald links. Continue with four more emerald links, ending at the clasp.

9. Attach a series of three emerald links at the back of the clasp, making sure to add the remaining vintage crystal dangle near the clasp. Attach the fob to the bottom loop of the last link.

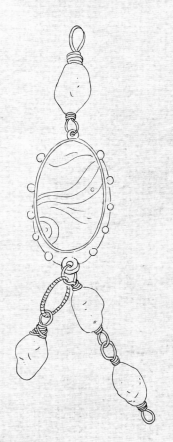

C. Detail of beads attached to bezel

JOURNAL Notes

For this piece, I used a modified complementary color scheme of red-violet and yellow-green. The emerald gemstone beads coordinate with the worn patina of the vintage bronze brooch, and the touch of "grape" color adds a nice accent.

Complementary schemes are very high contrast, will draw maximum attention to your design, and should be used wisely to avoid looking harsh. Combining pure hues of complementary colors is an especially vibrant look and should be carefully considered and used sparingly. Tones, tints, and shades, like I used here, are easier to manage in a complementary scheme. Using one color as the base and the other as an accent will help you achieve the right effect.

With this piece I also had to be careful about the physical balance. Both the resin-filled bezel and the large round lamp-work glass bead are fairly heavy. I balanced them on opposite sides so the necklace would hang properly. I also purposely used a bit of red-violet in the bezel image so the piece would be visually balanced. Careful placement of the violet helps draw the eye around the piece.

DESIGN Tips

- The emerald beads I used were a little more expensive, but the quality was not high, which kept the cost down. I prefer the muted and imperfect look of these emeralds as opposed to perfect ones. Their look is in keeping with my style and the found objects I used. Keep your style in mind when shopping for stones. Consider the look you are going for, and the stones and objects you are trying to combine.

- Lamp-work beads and elements are easy to find online. If you don't have lamp-work on hand, or prefer not to use it, you can always use gemstones or other beads in the right color.

- This fox brooch was gifted to me, and when I first received it I thought I might never use it. One day I picked it up and held the emeralds to it and I knew it was a great match. Some objects stay in my collection for years before I use them, but they finally find their place in a piece of jewelry. Typically, I weed out what I know I will never use, but I recommend keeping elements that are a possibility. You never know when the perfect strand of gemstones or pearls will come along, and inspire you to create a wonderful combination.

sacred Heart *Necklace*

TOOLS

- pliers; round-nose, chain-nose
- jewelry hammer
- rawhide mallet or dead-blow hammer
- bench block and bench pillow
- flush cut wire snips
- flush cutters such as Power Max
- metal file
- fine-grit foam sanding block
- awl
- flex-shaft, Dremel tool, or hand drill
- 1/16" (2 mm) titanium bit
- butane torch

MATERIALS

- sterling silver wire, 22-gauge
- sterling silver wire, 24- or 26-gauge
- purchased clasp
- bezel
- gloss gel medium
- resin kit such as ICE Resin
- vintage brooch
- one 10 mm faceted aquamarine briolette
- 3" (7.5 cm) vintage chain
- small filigree
- four 6 mm red pearls
- three small vintage rhinestone buttons
- vintage sacred heart scapular
- ten 6 mm gold pearls
- vintage magnifying glass
- 26" (66 cm) rhinestone chain
- eight 6 mm faceted garnets
- one 10 mm oval jump ring
- vintage disco-ball bead
- silver puffed heart
- vintage cross

INSTRUCTIONS

1. For the clasp, cut the image to fit, seal with gloss gel medium, and allow it to dry. Adhere the image inside the bezel with more gel medium. Mix the resin according to the package directions and fill the bezel; allow the resin to set at least twenty-four hours.

2. For the focal, snip the pin back from rhinestone brooch using the Power Max cutters; file and sand smooth. If necessary, remove rhinestones using an awl, and then drill holes as needed for the links at the top and bottom.

A. Close-up of rhinestone pin connections

B. Close-up of scapular with pearl link and magnifying glass

Necklace at full length

3. Using 24- or 26-gauge wire, wrap a briolette and attach it to the lower center of the brooch before closing the wrap.

4. Using 1" (2.5 cm) of chain for each side of the focal, attach one end to the focal lower corners and the other ends to the filigree (see A).

5. Use 22-gauge wire to make all the links. Make a wrapped link using a red pearl, threading two rhinestone buttons onto the top of the link before closing and attaching to the bottom of the filigree.

6. Drill a hole in the top of the scapular. Make a wrapped link using a gold pearl, and attach it to the bottom of the red link and the top of the scapular. Connect the magnifying glass at the top of the red link using a 1" (2.5 cm) length of chain (see B).

7. Cut two 13" (33 cm) lengths of rhinestone chain. Make four coil crimp ends, and attach one to each end of the rhinestone chains.

8. Attach the following above each side of the focal: one garnet link, two gold pearl links, one red pearl link, and one end of a rhinestone chain.

9. On the other end of rhinestone chain, attach two garnet links, and one gold pearl link. Attach the other end of the gold pearl links to the clasp and hook (see C).

10. Attach the jump ring to the hook part of the clasp. To this attach one gold pearl link, one garnet link, one red pearl link, and one disco ball link, ending with the puffed heart. Also attach one garnet link, two gold pearl links, and end with the cross, attaching the last rhinestone button before closing the final gold pearl link.

C. Side view of clasp

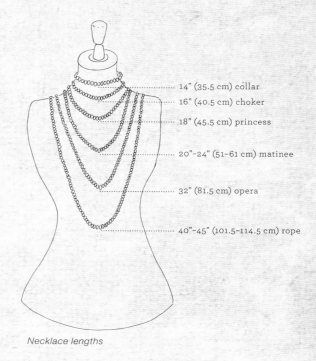

14" (35.5 cm) collar
16" (40.5 cm) choker
18" (45.5 cm) princess
20"–24" (51–61 cm) matinee
32" (81.5 cm) opera
40"–45" (101.5–114.5 cm) rope

Necklace lengths

JOURNAL Notes

This necklace measures about 39" (99 cm), which qualifies as "rope" length. It was meant to be worn either as one long strand or doubled with the clasp in the front at the throat, and with the puffed heart and cross dangling down as a secondary focal. Because there is a lot going on when it is worn this way, I deliberately kept the chain part of the necklace relatively plain and used a thin length of rhinestone cup chain.

This piece has no shortage of texture and I have used one of my favorite visual textures—sparkle. The rhinestones, faceted beads, and various elements added so much visual and physical texture, I thought it was best to keep the sizes of the beads and components delicate. The focal elements are also on the petite side to remain in proportion. The subtle sparkle and interesting textures make the viewer want to reach out and touch this necklace.

DESIGN Tips

- A scapular is a small badge, piece of cloth, or paper worn as a sign of devotion. You could use any number of found objects in its place, including a watch fob, rhinestone brooch, metal tag, doll's leg, or watch face. The magnifying glass was a fun addition and provided a way to get a closer look at the scapular.

- In place of the rhinestone chains, try using recycled sari silk, or a vintage chain.

- I used a purchased clasp for this piece. For a long necklace that can be worn doubled, I like to use a clasp that sits right side up whether it is worn in the back or front. This resin-filled bezel clasp is easily adjustable so it can be worn either way.

Adornment, what a science! Beauty, what a weapon! Modesty, what elegance!

—COCO CHANEL

CHAPTER 5
DESIGNING WITH BALANCE, PROPORTION, and FOCUS

BALANCE IS THE DISTRIBUTION of visual and physical weight in a piece. If the physical balance is off, the jewelry may be difficult to wear. If the visual balance is off, it will be difficult to look at!

Symmetrical designs are created by equally distributing like-components on either side of a focal, lending a sense of stability and a more formal feeling. The use of color can help reinforce symmetrical balance.

Asymmetrical designs are more informal, but can be more difficult to construct—the key is balance. The elements on either side of a design should combine in a harmonious way using both visual and physical balance. Divided down the center, an asymmetrical design should appear visually balanced with each element benefiting the overall design. Components don't have to match but they complement each other. Using only one or two colors helps unify asymmetrical designs. When carefully composed, asymmetry creates excitement and interest. Proportion is how the components and elements in your jewelry relate to each other, and as a whole. Being thoughtful of good proportion adds harmony and balance to your piece. If one element's size or shape is out of proportion, the eye will be drawn to the wrong place, and cause discord. Quantity, color, and placement also play a part. When designing, move elements around, or try different shapes and sizes until you find the right combination.

Focus is the most important feature of your piece, whether it is an interesting focal or an outstanding color, it will be the first place the eye lands. It is easy to select a focus; the tricky part is adding additional elements. You must establish a visual hierarchy—the main focus, possibly a secondary focal, and then supporting elements. If the piece is too busy, the eye becomes distracted. A secondary focal is never required, but it sometimes adds interest and should accent the main focal.

When working with found objects with unusual texture, patina, or shape, it's important to feature them in a way that is not distracting. Designers often try to include everything they love in one piece. Too many discordant elements will ruin the harmony—less is really more. A carefully balanced and proportionate piece, with a prominent, well-accented focal, will be beautiful to view, and will also communicate your idea in a cohesive way.

symmetrical:
REVERSIBLE STEAMPUNK *Necklace*

TOOLS

- pliers; toothed, round-nose, extra-long round-nose, chain-nose, bailing
- crimp tool
- jewelry hammer
- rawhide mallet or dead-blow hammer
- bench block and bench pillow
- flush cut wire snips
- metal file
- fine-grit foam sanding block
- scissors
- torch

MATERIALS

- copper wire, 14-gauge
- copper wire, 24-gauge
- medium-weight beading wire
- vintage pocket watch
- mica
- 16" (40.5 cm) strand 15–30 mm, graduated, unpolished amber beads
- twelve 10 mm vintage metal, round beads
- 2 mm sterling crimp tubes
- jewelry glue

DESIGN *Tips*

- Make sure to check amber before stringing, to be sure the pieces are stable and don't break when pressed firmly.

- After I popped the back off my watch, I filed down a pin that prevented the mica from lying flat. I don't usually use glue in my pieces, but this time it seemed like the easiest route to attach the mica. Make sure you have a good connection—use enough glue to affix the mica, but not so much that it overflows.

- Instead of making the large eye part of this clasp, you can use the hook with a regular wrapped link, as long as it is in proportion to the rest of the piece.

A. Detail of focal wire wrap

JOURNAL Notes

I found this amazing pocket watch while shopping with a good friend. She picked it up and commented that maybe I could do something with it. After closer examination, I really liked the worn face even though it was heavy and almost too weighty for a focal. When I got it home, it sat around for a while until I picked it up and noticed it was still ticking, even without the hands or a crystal. That is when I became intrigued. I had a design in mind that incorporated a compass, but felt this watch would work if I could remove its guts and reduce the weight. When I popped the back off, I discovered the large lovely gears were still intact. I decided not to remove them because I wanted to give the viewer a little surprise when the watch is turned over. The peek-a-boo element and design of the clasp and body of the necklace allow it to be reversible.

I selected large beads to be in proportion with the watch. The size and color of the amber balanced well with the watch, while the vintage metal beads blend in for just the right accent. The symmetrical design of this piece keeps the eye on the beauty of the focal.

INSTRUCTIONS

1. For the focal, remove the watch back, cut the mica to fit, and glue it to the watch back.

   Using 8" (20.5 cm) of 14-gauge wire, ball both ends, and then wrap loops at both ends, attaching the pocket watch to one end before closing the loop (see A).

2. For the clasp, use 3½" (9 cm) of 14-gauge wire, ball one end, and then shape the hook part of the clasp. For the eye component, use 4½" (11.5 cm) of 14-gauge wire, paddle both ends, and then wrap loops using the back of the extra-long round-nose pliers. Use bailing pliers to shape a large loop, and hammer the loop flat. Using the back of the extra-long round-nose pliers and 14-gauge wire, make a jump ring, and then flatten it. Attach the jump ring to the small loops using 24-gauge wire, and wrap the wire around the base of the large loop. Flatten all 24-gauge wraps (see B).

3. String amber and metal beads onto the beading wire, placing the watch at the center. Then attach the wire ends to the hook and eye with crimp tubes (see C).

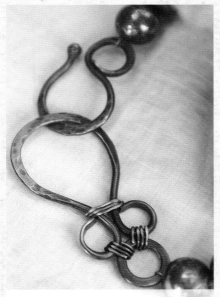

B. Close-up of clasp

Close-up of focal back

Close-up of focal

C. Reverse side of focal

symmetrical:
NIGHT GARDEN *Necklace*

TOOLS

- pliers; round-nose, extra-long round-nose, chain-nose, bailing
- jewelry hammer
- rawhide mallet or dead-blow hammer
- bench block and bench pillow
- flush cut wire snips
- compound flush cutters such as Power Max
- metal file
- fine-grit foam sanding block
- flex-shaft or Dremel tool and bits
- awl

MATERIALS

- sterling wire, 22-gauge
- sterling wire, 24-gauge
- sterling wire, 26-gauge
- one large vintage rhinestone brooch
- one 3 mm rhinestone rondelle
- one 12 mm briolette garnet bead
- one large vintage rhinestone clasp
- eighteen 2–3 mm red pearls
- fourteen 18 mm faceted tourmaline beads
- seven 6 mm round faceted garnet beads
- one vintage rhinestone drop
- jewelry glue

DESIGN *Tips*

- This symmetrical design is great because you can use any color beads and the focus remains on the brooch. The bead sizes should be fairly large to stay in proportion with the large rhinestone focal.

- For this necklace I kept the length short so the focal lies near the face. If you would like a longer necklace, just add more links.

- This brooch was missing some rhinestones and I didn't have the right shapes in my stash to replace all of them. It doesn't bother me to have a few missing stones, and I think it adds to the vintage appeal of the piece.

A. Close-up of focal with wrapped briolette

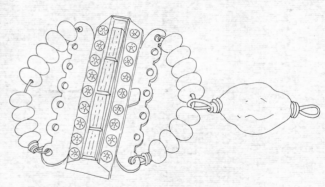

B. Close-up of clasp

C. Rhinestone drop

INSTRUCTIONS

1. For the focal, remove the pin back from the rhinestone brooch; file and sand smooth. Use jewelry glue to replace any missing rhinestones. Using the awl, remove rhinestones if necessary, and drill holes to attach links and a drop.

2. For the drop use 24- or 26-gauge wire and a rhinestone rondelle to create a link; attach it to the brooch. Wrap a briolette bead using 24- or 26-gauge wire and attach it to the rondelle link before closing the loop (see A).

3. For the clasp, cut about 3" (7.5 cm) of 26-gauge wire and attach one end to the clasp by making a small loop. Thread pearls onto the wire and attach the other end to the clasp with a small loop. Repeat for the other side of the clasp (see B).

4. Create links using 22-gauge wire and the tourmaline beads. Attach the links together, joining the ends to the brooch and clasp on each side of the necklace.

5. Create links using 22-gauge wire and the garnet beads, attaching them together and to the back of the clasp. Attach the rhinestone drop before closing the final link (see C).

JOURNAL Note

This is a design I originally created to go with a holiday sweater. The first necklace was made with blue chalcedony beads and a lovely flower rhinestone brooch. I liked the design so much that I wanted to repeat it, and when I found this gorgeous old brooch in a similar style I knew exactly what I wanted to do. The brooch is quite large, and not wanting to distract from it I kept the rest of the necklace relatively simple and symmetrical. The symmetrical design conveys a classical, elegant feeling that perfectly accents the rhinestone piece. Of course I couldn't resist adding a bit of bling at the back with a strand made from garnets and a vintage rhinestone drop in my favorite gemstone shape—an emerald-cut.

Detail of vintage rhinestone brooch

asymmetrical:
messenger *Necklace*

TOOLS

- pliers; toothed, round-nose, extra-long round-nose, chain-nose, bailing
- crimp tool
- jewelry hammer
- rawhide mallet or dead-blow hammer
- bench block and bench pillow
- flush cut wire snips
- fine-grit foam sanding block
- scissors
- torch
- sewing needle

MATERIALS

- sterling wire, 14-gauge
- sterling wire, 22-gauge
- sterling wire, 24- or 26-gauge
- medium-weight beading wire
- vintage paper
- one purchased bezel
- white glue
- small dried floral element
- two-part resin such as ICE Resin
- vintage fabric element
- upholstery thread
- one 4 mm jump ring
- three 4 mm vintage crystal beads
- one 11 mm garnet briolette bead
- 3" (7.5 cm) of vintage chain
- three 12 mm baroque pearls
- twenty-eight 7 mm faceted rondelle peridot beads
- two 10 mm faceted round garnet beads
- two 14 mm faceted oval rutilated quartz beads
- vintage crucifix
- vintage lace
- one 15 mm jump ring
- 2 mm sterling crimp tubes

Close-up of crucifix

INSTRUCTIONS

1. For the resin-filled bezel, affix paper to the bottom of the bezel using white glue on the edges. Also affix a small floral element inside the bezel. Fill the bezel with resin following the package instructions; allow the resin to set for twenty-four hours.

2. For the focal, stitch a 4 mm jump ring onto the bottom. Create a crystal link and attach one end to a garnet-wrapped briolette and the other end to the jump ring of the focal. Make a pearl drop and attach it with a chain to the jump ring. Make a peridot link and attach one end to the crucifix and the other end to the jump ring. Also tie a short length of lace to the jump ring (see A).

3. For the clasp, ball both ends of 5" (12.5 cm) 14-gauge wire, and create two loops for the eye. For the hook, use 4" (10 cm) of 14-gauge wire, ball both ends, and make a loop at one end and a hook at the other.

4. On one side of necklace, use 8" (20.5 cm) of 22-gauge wire and five peridot beads to create a long link, and attach it to the bezel. Onto beading wire, string a crimp tube, a crystal bead, twelve peridot beads, a quartz bead, and another crimp tube; attach one end to the bezel and the other end to the closure hook. Sew the peridot link to the focal.

5. For the other side of the necklace, make links using a garnet, pearl, and pearl, in that order and join them together. Sew the garnet link onto the focal, and attach the pearl link onto a large jump ring. On the other side of jump ring, attach a quartz link. To the quartz link, string a crimp tube, nine peridot beads, one garnet bead, and a crimp tube, in that order. Attach one end to the quartz link and the other end to the eye part of the closure.

6. Cut 3" (7.5 cm) of 22-gauge wire, and ball one end to make a drop. Add a peridot bead and create a loop, attaching it to the large jump ring before closing.

asymmetrical design Tips

· Divide your asymmetrical design in half with an imaginary line. Is it visually balanced on each side?

· Consider every element. Is it beneficial to the design? If the design is as good without it—don't add it. Remember, components don't have to match but they must go together.

· Use only one or two colors to help unify asymmetrical designs.

· Try on the piece to test for physical balance. Does it hang properly or do you need to continually readjust it?

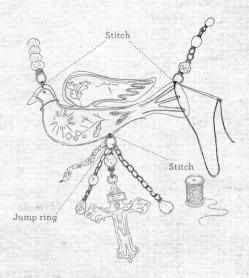

A. Detail of focal

Close-up of focal back

JOURNAL Notes

This is one of my all-time favorite pieces. The focal is a vintage religious piece made from fabric, which is called a détente. I was very lucky to pick up this beautiful dove in a lot that I purchased online. The dove is seen as a symbol of love and peace as well as a messenger. I frequently use asymmetrical designs in my work, and I didn't want to distract from this special focal, so I drew a palette from the colors in the embroidery, and kept the colors and elements visually balanced. I was also careful to keep all of the elements in proportion, resulting in a physically balanced and harmonious necklace.

DESIGN Tips

· If you can't find a vintage fabric détente, or don't want a religious piece, you can always stitch your own focal. This dove is basically a little embroidered pillow. When I first got it, some of the embroidery was coming loose, so I reinforced it with small stitches that blended into the background. I also reinforced the beadwork.

· Asymmetrical designs typically have more going on than symmetrical designs so you must think about each component carefully. Each item should be chosen to accent the focal and not stand out too much. Pay close attention to size, proportion, and balance, and then use color as a unifying element.

asymmetrical:
a walk in the city Necklace

TOOLS

- pliers; round-nose, chain-nose
- crimp tool
- jewelry hammer
- rawhide mallet or dead-blow hammer
- bench block and bench pillow
- flush cut wire snips
- fine-grit foam sanding block
- scissors

MATERIALS

- sterling wire, 20-gauge
- sterling wire, 22-gauge
- medium-weight beading wire
- one vintage beveled glass element
- small amount of upholstery fabric
- white glue or gel medium
- two 17 mm pearls
- six 10 mm square, faceted amethyst beads
- one 15 mm faceted amethyst bead
- one vintage rhinestone clasp
- two 16" (40.5 cm) strands 4 mm, faceted amethyst heishi beads
- 2 mm sterling crimp tubes
- one vintage religious connector
- one rhinestone drop
- one vintage shoe charm

A. Close-up of focal back

B. Close-up of focal

C. Close-up of pearl and religious connector

INSTRUCTIONS

1. For the focal, cut a rectangle of fabric and adhere it to the back of the beveled-glass piece with glue or gel medium (see A). Using 20-gauge wire, make a small hook at one end. Thread the wire through the metal trim across the upper edge of the beveled piece, and make another small hook at the other end; bend the hooks up (see B).

2. On one side of the necklace, make four links using 22-gauge wire, a pearl, and three square amethyst beads. Connect the pearl link to the focal and the three amethyst links to the pearl. Make a link with the faceted amethyst nugget and connect it to the clasp. Using beading wire, thread a crimp, 4" (10 cm) of heishi, and then connect the wire to the square amethyst links on one end and amethyst nugget link on the other end.

3. For other side of the necklace, make a pearl link and connect it to the focal and religious connector (see C). String two strands of heishi, each about 6" (15 cm) long onto beading wire. Connect the wire to the religious connector and clasp.

4. Connect a rhinestone drop to the clasp. Make and connect links made with the remaining square amethyst beads, connect the top at the clasp, and add a shoe charm to the bottom (see D).

D. Close-up of stones and charm at the clasp

I had purchased a lovely glass jewelry box that was partially falling apart. When the top came off, I immediately thought, "What a great focal." I'm not sure what city is depicted under the bezel, but it looks like a wonderful place for a walk. I added the shoe charm to represent that stroll.

This design is technically asymmetrical but with a very symmetrical look. Using amethyst heishi on both sides helps keep the piece visually balanced. I added the square beads and nugget of amethyst to help with physical balance. The sparkle of the heishi adds a lot of texture and interest without being overpowering.

DESIGN Tips

- If you can't find a similar jewelry box top, try using a chandelier crystal for your focal.

- To make the back of the bezel prettier and more durable, I affixed a rectangle of thick fabric in a coordinating color.

- When you are designing asymmetrically, make sure you balance the piece physically. If you use a heavy element on one side, make sure it is balanced on the other side by something of similar weight.

PHYSICAL BALANCE:
e PLURIBUS UNUM *Bracelet*

TOOLS

- pliers; round-nose, chain-nose, bailing
- jewelry hammer
- rawhide mallet or dead-blow hammer
- bench block and bench pillow
- flush cut wire snips
- compound flush cutters such as Power Max
- metal file
- fine-grit foam sanding block
- flex-shaft or Dremel tool and bits
- center punch
- awl

MATERIALS

- sterling wire, 14-gauge
- sterling wire, 20-gauge
- vintage military hat badge
- vintage rhinestone earring
- vintage wooden bingo token
- one 15 mm bone ring
- one 28 mm faceted prehnite bead
- one 18 mm round vintage metal bead
- vintage metal charm
- one vintage rhinestone drop
- one 4 mm jump ring

DESIGN *Tip*

The key to this bracelet's good design is carefully choosing a melodious mixture of properly proportioned objects. Each item is interesting in its own right, which makes for a fascinating piece of jewelry! Choose meaningful objects from your collection and move them around before linking them together permanently. Trying different arrangements will help you get the design perfect.

A. Close-up of rhinestone earring

B. Close-up of bingo token

C. Close-up of focal

D. Close-up of clasp

INSTRUCTIONS

1. For the focal, remove the badge back; file and sand smooth. Mark holes at the sides with a center punch, and then drill.

2. Using an awl, remove any rhinestones from the earring if necessary, and drill holes for the links. Make a link and attach it to one side of the earring, and then connect the other side to the focal (see A).

3. Drill a hole through the bingo token, and then use it to create a link. Attach the token to the earring and bone ring (see B).

4. Make a clasp from 3" (7.5 cm) of 14-gauge wire.

5. Create a link with the prehnite bead, and attach it to the opposite side of the focal (see C).

6. Make a link with the metal bead, and connect it to the prehnite link and clasp.

7. Using a jump ring, connect the metal charm and rhinestone drop to the clasp (see D).

Size and proportion are important with a simple design.

JOURNAL *Notes*

The focal for this bracelet is a splendid vintage badge from a U.S. military hat. It really appeals to the patriotic part of me, and the design proves that sometimes less is more. There is a lot of texture happening here, so I kept the color scheme fairly neutral.

   With only five components to the main part of the bracelet, the design is deceptively simple. In reality, I spent some time choosing just the right elements. It is important for the parts to be in proportion to live harmoniously together. The focal is rather large, so the other components needed to be somewhat large as well. After trying on the bracelet, I added the charm and rhinestone drop at the clasp to help balance the weight so it would hang properly on the arm. Now this piece is visually and physically balanced.

PHYSICAL BALANCE:
POMPEII BARS AND RODS Earrings

TOOLS

- pliers; toothed, round-nose, chain-nose, bailing
- jewelry hammer
- rawhide mallet or dead-blow hammer
- bench block and bench pillow
- flush cut wire snips
- metal shears
- metal file
- fine-grit foam sanding block
- center punch
- flex-shaft, Dremel tool, or hand drill
- 1/16" (2 mm) titanium bit
- butane torch

MATERIALS

- sterling silver wire, 20-gauge
- metal trim, textured metal, or filigree
- four 8 mm pearls

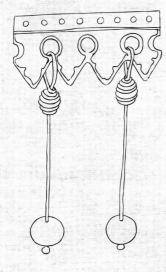

A. Drill holes for ear wire and dangles.

INSTRUCTIONS

1. Cut the metal trim into two pieces; file the edges. If it is necessary to drill holes, use the center punch to mark their placement. Drill three holes in each metal piece, two for the dangles and one for the ear wire (see A).

2. For each of four dangles, ball one end of a 3" (7.5 cm) piece of 20-gauge wire. Thread a pearl onto the wire, and then make a loop at the other end. Connect the loop to the metal trim before completing the wrap.

3. Ball one end of another piece of 20-gauge wire, and create an ear wire; attach it to the metal trim. Repeat for the second earring.

Know, first, who you are, and then adorn yourself accordingly.

—EPICTETUS

CHAPTER 6

DESIGNING WITH
RHYTHM and HARMONY

RHYTHM AND HARMONY go hand in hand and are related to movement and unity. When considering rhythm and movement in your designs, think about the way your eye is drawn around a piece. The eye should first be drawn to the focal, and then up or around the piece to the less important elements. The pattern can be regular or irregular, symmetrical or asymmetrical, but the eye should be easily guided. The arrangement of components should also evoke a pleasing cadence. Repeated elements, patterns, or colors are a great way to create easy rhythm.

Rhythm and movement are not strictly visual. Physical movement can be an important aspect in your designs. If the jewelry includes many swinging objects or charms, it is important to ensure the piece is physically balanced as well.

The final objective for your designs is for them to be harmonious and unified. The number of elements is unimportant, as long as they relate to each other in an agreeable and pleasing arrangement. Creating a harmonious and unified design is like singing a beautiful song; if one note is harsh or out of tune, it is quite noticeable! Components and colors do not necessarily have to match, but they should go together. Each element should complement other similar elements and enhance contrasting elements. All of the parts should combine together to create a cohesive and beautiful whole.

DOG LOVER'S CHARM *Bracelet*

TOOLS

- pliers; toothed, round-nose, extra-long round-nose, bailing, chain-nose
- flush cut wire snips
- compound flush cutters, such as Power Max
- metal file
- fine-grit foam sanding block
- flex-shaft or Dremel tool
- drill bits
- torch

MATERIALS

- sterling silver wire, 22-gauge
- six or seven vintage dog pins or charms
- four vintage dog tags
- one 15 mm stone-heart charm
- eight 6 mm crystal rondelles
- four 9 mm faceted rubies
- vintage rhinestone bracelet
- four 10 mm crystal beads
- seven 6 mm crystal beads

DESIGN *Tips*

- When using so many charms, physical balance must be considered in this design. Placing the heaviest charm in the center and an equally heavy one near the clasp helps keep the weight evenly distributed so the bracelet doesn't list to one side when worn.

- A variety of small objects can be used as charms for this bracelet. Try using vintage rhinestone earrings, game pieces, watch faces, tintypes, coins, or nearly anything that can be drilled.

INSTRUCTIONS

1. Prepare the dog pins by removing the pin backs or other findings with the power cutters; file smooth. Carefully drill holes in, or near the heads.

2. Lay out an arrangement of the dog charms so that the largest and heaviest is centered on the bracelet (see A), and the next heaviest is near the clasp. Intersperse the remaining dog charms and stone-heart charm evenly with the dog tags.

A. Place the heaviest charm in the center.

B. Detail of charm connection

3. Make four balled head pins and thread each with a crystal rondelle, a ruby, and a second crystal rondelle. Place these in the arrangement, filling in empty spots in the design.

4. Attach all charms to the rhinestone bracelet using wrapped links (see B). Use small crystal beads with dog charms and large crystal beads with the tags and stone heart (see C).

C. Attach charms between links of bracelet.

JOURNAL *Notes*

Charms have been a part of personal adornment since ancient times. People have worn them as personal expressions of faith, as amulets, talismans, and lucky charms to ward off evil. Charm bracelets became popular when Queen Victoria of Great Britain often wore them. She made them a style statement, and they have remained popular in various forms ever since. For this bracelet, I parted ways with tradition, and used a vintage rhinestone bracelet as the base instead of a chain.

This sentimental charm bracelet was made in memory of my little fox terrier, Maggie. I had been collecting vintage terrier pins for a long time, and when I looked for her dog tag I found that I had four! Each one was either in the shape of a heart or was engraved with hearts—the work of my (Wife Whisperer) husband.

Close-up of charms

amethyst medallion *Necklace*

TOOLS

- pliers; round-nose, extra-long round-nose, bailing, chain-nose
- jewelry hammer
- bench block and bench pillow
- flush cut wire snips
- fine-grit foam sanding block

MATERIALS

- sterling silver wire, 22-gauge
- four 5 mm garnet beads
- vintage rhinestone clasp
- jump ring
- vintage medallion or brooch
- 12" (30.5 cm) vintage chain
- large vintage jump ring
- vintage crucifix
- two vintage metal findings (or a metal bead and stamping)
- six 14–20 mm faceted tourmaline beads
- 6" (15 cm) vintage rosary chain
- vintage religious medal

Detail of vintage religious medal

INSTRUCTIONS

1. Create four links with the small garnet beads, and connect two to each side the clasp; set aside.

2. Connect two, 1" (2.5 cm) lengths of chain to the lower corners of the medallion, and connect the other ends to the large jump ring (see A).

3. Attach the crucifix to one end of the vintage metal finding or bead, and attach the finding to the bottom of the jump ring (see B).

C. Vintage filigree connection

A. Join chains to the medallion and large jump ring.

B. Close-up of vintage metal bead and crucifix

4. Make three links using the larger tourmaline beads. Connect two links to the upper right corner of the medallion.

5. Connect two 1" (2.5 cm) chains to the upper large tourmaline link, and attach the opposite ends to the corners of the metal finding or stamping.

6. On the same side, connect two 2½" (6.5 cm) lengths of chain to the top of the finding (see C). Connect the chain's opposite ends to the links on one side of the clasp with a jump ring.

7. On the other side of the necklace, connect the remaining large gemstone link to the medallion's upper left corner. Connect the rosary beads/chain to the link.

8. Using one of the larger beads, make a wrapped link. Attach one side to the opposite end of the rosary chain, and the other side to the smaller beads attached to the clasp.

9. Make wrapped links from the remaining two larger beads, connect the links, and then attach them to the necklace near the clasp. Connect the religious medal to the link's other end (see D).

D. Close-up of clasp with link connections

DESIGN Tips

• You may not have the luck to stumble across a Victorian belt, but don't worry; a vintage necklace, or elements from disparate places will work just as well. Shop with an eye for what you can do with an element or two from a whole necklace, bracelet, or earrings. Once you take apart a piece of jewelry, you may find yourself with a wealth of elements to play with.

• I like to use vintage crosses and crucifixes for their beauty and meaning. If you'd rather not use a religious element, try a large faceted, top-drilled briolette bead instead.

• I used vintage chain, but new chain will work as well. There are many patina products on the market to help get an aged look.

JOURNAL Notes

On one of my many treasure hunts I discovered a gorgeous Victorian belt containing six of these amazing medallions with beautiful purple cut-glass stones. The medallions were interspersed with chain, metal stampings, and filigree beads; lots of material for jewelry making. I immediately envisioned a series of necklaces from this lovely piece.

You don't see elements like these every day, and your work will have much more interest and appeal if you use a unique focal and one-of-a-kind findings. Because this focal is so eye-catching, I used a monochromatic color scheme to create a harmonious look and allow the medallion to stand out.

It can be tricky to design an asymmetrical piece with a rhythmic and harmonious look, especially when you have a standout focal like this one—balance is key. To visually balance this necklace, I combined a vintage filigree with chains on one side. On the other side, I used color (violet rosary beads) to create interest. These elements balance each other, enabling the eye to see the focal first, and then easily move up the rest of the piece in a rhythmic way.

TRINITY *Earrings*

TOOLS

- pliers; toothed, round-nose, chain-nose, bailing
- jewelry hammer
- rawhide mallet or dead-blow hammer
- bench block and bench pillow
- flush cut wire snips
- fine-grit foam sanding block
- butane torch

MATERIALS

- sterling silver wire, 20-gauge
- sterling silver wire, 22-gauge
- sterling silver wire, 24- or 26-gauge
- two 7 mm vintage crystal beads
- two vintage religious connectors
- eight 4 mm faceted garnet beads
- two 3 mm round garnet beads
- two 4 mm crystal beads

INSTRUCTIONS

1. Using 22-gauge wire and a 7 mm crystal, make a wire link with loops at both ends.

2. Using 24- or 26-gauge wire (depending on which size fits through the beads) make a small loop at one end, attaching it to the religious connector. Thread four 4 mm garnet beads onto the wire, add the crystal link, and then four more garnets. Bend the wire end to create another loop shape, and connect the loop to other side of religious connector (see A).

Trinity earrings with tourmaline

A. Detail of earring construction

3. Using 24- or 26-gauge wire, make a beaded head pin, and thread on a 3 mm round garnet bead and a 4 mm crystal bead. Make a loop at the top, and join it to bottom of religious connector.

4. Using 20-gauge wire, make two ear wires. Ball one end and flatten it before shaping the ear wires. Attach them to the earrings, and then close the ear wires securely.

JOURNAL Note

Vintage religious connectors are a staple of my found object designs. The three-point connection makes them very versatile and easy to design with.

DESIGN Tips

- If you don't want to use religious connectors, it's relatively easy to get other types of findings. I used vintage brass stampings for the amethyst Trinity earrings, but you could use new.

- These earrings are easy to design in different ways. For the garnet pair, I used a wrapped link at the top. For the others I connected the beaded loop directly to the ear wire. You could also join a rhinestone drop to the bottom point of the connector, instead of the head pin with beads.

- These earrings look terrific with all kinds of colors and gemstones. The stones don't have to be faceted or transparent. You could try this design with turquoise, or even seed beads. Select beads at about 5 mm or less to prevent the earrings from becoming too chunky.

SPIRITS *Necklace*

TOOLS

- pliers; round-nose, chain-nose
- flush cut wire snips
- flush cutters such as Power Max
- metal file
- fine-grit foam sanding block
- flex-shaft, Dremel tool, or hand drill
- $\frac{1}{16}$" (2 mm) titanium bit

MATERIALS

- sterling silver wire, 24- or 26-gauge
- one vintage rosary with small religious connector
- one small vintage rhinestone clasp
- one, 3 mm crystal dangle
- eight, 10 mm jump rings
- 2"–3" (5–7.5 cm) vintage chain
- two small vintage religious medals
- eight vintage black glass and rhinestone buttons
- five large vintage religious medals
- one, 15 mm pyrite briolette
- one vintage rhinestone earring
- one vintage small rhinestone buckle
- three vintage crosses
- one vintage pocket saint

INSTRUCTIONS

1. Separate the links at the back of the rosary, and connect the ends to either side of the clasp. Attach the 3 mm crystal dangle to the clasp. Attach the rosary chain at either side of the clasp.

2. For the focal, use a jump ring to attach one large medal and one black-glass button below the religious connector.

3. Using 24- or 26-gauge wire, wrap a briolette, and set aside.

A. Detail of necklace configuration

B. Close-up of charm layout

C. Buckle with medallion and button

D. Detail of wrapped briolette

E. Close-up of chain link attachment

4. Prepare the earring by removing the findings; file and sand if necessary. Drill a hole in the top of the earring if needed.

5. Prepare the buckle by removing any findings; file and sand.

6. Lay out an arrangement of medals, crosses, and other elements including the briolette, earring, and buckle. Space the elements, balancing them on either side of the necklace (see A).

7. Stack elements in groups of three. Place the largest in the back, and finish with a black-glass button at the front. Make six stacks, and use a jump ring to attach each group to the necklace (see B, C, and D). Use a few links from the chain to attach charms, if necessary (see E). Make sure all the jump rings are closed tightly.

JOURNAL Notes

This necklace is loaded with some of my favorite objects. It is a very versatile and can easily be personalized to include things you have in your stash. It can be worn with my "Dia de los Muertos Necklace" (page 89, and was designed so the focal of the Dia de los Muertos necklace would lie directly on top of the small rosary connector. Both pieces fit together nicely, and all of the elements can be seen. Originally, I created these pieces as one necklace, but I like flexibility, so I separated them so they can be worn either together or separately.

This necklace has a charm-bracelet style. At first, it may seem like the objects are a bit jumbled, but they were placed with much care. Planning the design is important so the many elements are physically and visually balanced. The objective was for this piece to be easy, interesting, and fun to view—not confusing or overwhelming. Careful placement ensures a rhythmic and harmonious whole.

DESIGN Tips

· The necklace length can easily be adjusted to be shorter or longer, depending on the look you are after. To shorten, remove some of the rosary chain, or make it longer by adding another rosary. The rosary links are fairly easy to open and close, but don't overwork them, or they may break.

· Remember to consider the necklace's wearability. I limited the weight of the necklace because I like to wear it with a heavier necklace. I used lightweight medals, and the pocket saint is plastic.

· Since I designed this to go with another piece, I added a bit of color, which coordinates nicely with the colors in its sister piece. The pocket saint, one of the crosses, and the sterling and enamel heart feature pink and raspberry hues, which add an interesting pop of color even when the piece is worn alone.

Resources

BEADS AND OBJECTS

Beads by Sandy: www.beadsbysandy.com

Ebay: www.ebay.com

Etsy: www.etsy.com

Happy Mango Beads: www.happymangobeads.com

METAL AND WIRE

Ace Hardware: www.acehardware.com

Fundametals: www.fundametals.net

Thunderbird Supply Company:
www.thunderbirdsupply.com

TOOLS AND SUPPLIES

The Antique Palette (bench pillows): www.etsy.com/
shop/TheAntiquePalette

Contenti: www.contenti.com

Otto Frei: www.ottofrei.com

Rio Grande: www.riogrande.com

Volcano Arts: www.volcanoarts.com

acknowledgments

First, thanks to He who gives me strength to do all things.

Love to my guys for all of your encouragement, and for the times you reminded me not to take myself too seriously. Thank you for being my cheerleaders and my blessing; you rock.

Dad, I still remember all of those evenings of candle making and macramé. Thank you for helping me through the rough times; xxoo.

Mom, you have been one of my best creative mentors. Thank you for giving me your love of making things. You made me the treasure hunter I am today. I adore you.

Thank you Mary Ann Hall, and everyone at Quarry, for believing in me, answering my gazillion questions, and allowing me the creative freedom to express myself in this book.

To my sweet friends, thank you for supporting me, and loving me just the way I am.

Maggie, you taught me about joy. Mayzie, you're teaching me about gentleness.

Finally, thank you David, for slaying all of my Goliaths. Whisper on …

about deryn

Originally from Oregon, with a stop in Wyoming, Deryn Mentock got to Texas as fast as she could. There she wrangles a husband, two grown young men, an energetic pup, and a nice collection of cowboy boots. She has been passionate about art, especially jewelry design, for as long as she can remember. When she's not traveling to teach or treasure hunting, she is in the studio designing pieces that combine metal, gemstones, and unique well-loved treasures in unexpected ways. It is important to her that each piece is infused with color, texture, and her own spirit of faith and creativity. She is a nationally recognized instructor who loves teaching technique and design, as well as sharing insight into her creative process. She also enjoys teaching online workshops from the "Jewelry Works" page on the web. Her work includes designs for Michaels stores nationwide, and Susan Lenart Kazmer. Her jewelry and artwork have been featured in numerous books and magazines, including a feature article and cover for *Belle Armoire Jewelry.*

You can see more of Deryn's work on her blog, somethingsublime.typepad.com; her online workshop at somethingsublime.typepad.com/jewelry_works; and her online shop, mocknet.etsy.com.